The Green Wellie Guide

The Green Wellie Guide

Graham Nown

Cartoons by Mike Williams

Ward Lock Limited · London

© Graham Nown 1984

First published in Great Britain in paperback in 1987
by Ward Lock Limited, 8 Clifford Street,
London W1X 1RB, an Egmont Company

Text set in Palatino
by Fakenham Photosetting Limited
Fakenham, Norfolk

Printed and bound in Great Britain by
Hollen Street Press Limited

British Library Cataloguing in Publication Data

Nown, Graham
    The Green wellie guide.
    1. Etiquette – Great Britain – Anecdotes,
    satire, etc.
    I. Title   II. Nown, Sylvana
    395'.0941   BJ1874

    ISBN 0-7063-6587-9

Contents

Acknowledgments

Special thanks to Elizabeth Bowen-Jones, who provided the inspiration for this book, and to Robin Wood for his support and enthusiasm.

Thanks also to Dennis Alcock, Richard Compton Miller, Babs Cort, Nicholas Courtney, author of *Sporting Royals* (Stanley Paul), Debrett's Peerage, David and Pauline Hampson-Smith, Tony Hazzard, Norman Hudson, Roddy Llewellyn and Alister Reid for their help . . . not forgetting the ubiquitous Hunter-Buckles, without whom this book would not have been possible.

To Rosie (Green Wellie size 3½)

How green are your wellies?

Your hostess, visibly pale, takes you discreetly to one side and informs you that the butler has summoned the bomb disposal squad after hearing an electronic buzzing coming from the locked suitcase in your bedroom. Horrified, you remember the vibrator Nigel packed as a practical joke.

Do you:

(a) Coolly explain that the office is bleeping, and ask if you can use the telephone.

(b) Give the offending device to your hostess as a house-gift.

or (c) Tell everyone they have two minutes to clear the building, and escape in the confusion.

You are moving forward in a line of walking guns. There is a rustle in the undergrowth. Instinctively you give a left and right, only to stumble upon your host lying on the ground, very dead.

Do you:

(a) Cover the body with leaves and move on.

(b) Stuff a scribbled note of apology into his Barbour pocket and run.

or (c) Offer the keeper a fiver to put him in the car boot of a disagreeable fellow guest.

You arrive by helicopter the day before your hostess opens her gardens to the public for a local charity. The down-draught removes every rose petal in sight, leaving a forest of bare thorns.

Do you:

(a) Crawl around trying desperately to stuff them all into your suitcase.

(b) Whistle loudly and remark how dreadful the weather is for the time of year.

or (c) Suggest brightly that enormous pot-pourri are terribly fashionable at the moment.

As you greet your host, his new rottweiler—recommended by the local crime prevention department—seizes your hand in its teeth and wrestles you to the floor.

Do you:

(a) Apologize profusely for causing it distress.

(b) Strangle it with your bare hands, and continue as though nothing had happened.

or (c) Ignore the incident, but spend the rest of the weekend with both arms plunged into a pair of Hendon Police College training muffs.

During dinner you notice that your trousers are unfastened. You zip them halfway up, but the corner of your large damask napkin becomes inextricably caught in your fly. As everyone rises, do you:

(a) Stuff it into your trousers to give the appearance of an enormous appendage.

(b) Leave it trailing to your knees and give Masonic signals.

or (c) Pretend nothing is amiss, and ostentatiously use it to clean your spectacles.

You tie a Thunder and Lightning and cast flamboyantly into the Dee, plucking your hostess's Hermes scarf from her head. She watches in mute surprise as it floats gently downstream.

The new rottweiler — recommended by the local crime prevention department — seizes your arm in its teeth and wrestles you to the floor.

Do you:

(a) Plunge in and chivalrously retrieve it.

(b) Knot the corners of your handkerchief and offer it to her as a replacement.

or (c) Remark casually that it is one of the Queen Mother's favourite flies, and you are feeling lucky today.

While hunting you are thrown headlong into a ditch, breaking a leg. The MFH, a prominent surgeon, takes command and rips your breeches up the seam to examine your injuries. The assembled field observes, in disbelief, that you are wearing nylon paisley Y-fronts.

Do you:

(a) Swear vehemently that you have never seen them before in your life.

(b) Confess, 'OK, squire, it's a fair cop.'

or (c) Explain that they are Lacoste, actually, but the motif must have become detached in the fall.

While partnering a bishop at bridge, you notice him surreptitiously draw a card from his gaiter.

Do you:

(a) Nudge him with your foot and wink encouragingly.

(b) Stand up and announce that he is a bounder and an overdressed tart.

or (c) Slip out your own concealed card and, if challenged, demand that he turns out his gaiters.

After a surfeit of excellent port you climb into bed, before the sobering truth dawns that it is not only the wrong room, but occupied.

Do you:

(a) Exit rapidly, pause, then rush back in to ask what all the screaming is about.

(b) Insist that it was a genuine mistake and assure her

that you will never reveal that she sleeps with her teeth in a glass of Sterodent.

or (c) Press a finger to her lips, and beg her to hide you. When she asks why, explain that your host is standing naked in your wardrobe.

The party is going well. You sit at the piano and idly vamp half a dozen bars of *Moonlight Sonata*. It is the only piece you know, and you have been practising day and night for the occasion. Your hostess's daughter, clearly impressed, begs you to play something else.

Do you:

(a) Lurch into a crippled rendering of *Chopsticks*.

(b) Quietly lower the lid, and say mysteriously: 'I'm sorry, my dear. People always ask, but the memories are still too painful.'

or (c) Reply 'Rather pretty, isn't it? One of the family wrote it—on the German side, of course . . .'

The weekend starts here

The Great British Country Weekend is a microcosm of everything true Brits of yeoman stock hold dear: sex, hard drinking, animals and utter eccentricity. Green Wellies, brought up to slosh around in the mud, share large, draughty houses with damp dogs, and play boisterous games designed to inflict maximum discomfort on strangers, find it nothing short of unbounded bliss. For the uninitiated, however, it is akin to a two-day assault course requiring the constitution of an elephant, and the training of an SAS sergeant. Hapless townies arrive totally unprepared for the gastric pummelling from gamey food, houses like Smithfield cold stores, and the terrifying ordeal of enormous, crotch-sniffing animals.

Anyone *au courant* with the quirky architecture of cavernous houses endowed with their own micro-climate, knows that waterproof, gale-proof country clothes were made to be worn indoors. Most of these houses were designed by architects heavily under the influence of port, who had no idea of the sheer hell future generations would have to go through simply to keep the blood circulating between Friday night and Sunday afternoon.

On Friday evenings the heaving watering-holes of SW7 are strangely eerie as the last round-up gets under way and herds of Hoorays and their Henriettas thunder to the country.

The pound and the price of smoked salmon may go up and down like a lavatory seat at Paddington station, but home on the Grange little changes. The Great British Country Weekend rolls on with a comforting, timeless regularity:

Arrive: Climb echoing stairs to be shown your bedroom. You turn up your collar at the icy blast from the chimney and calculate how much fuel the bedside pile of Dick Francis might produce, in an emergency. Only thirty-six hours to go . . . Downstairs again. Sip sherry, perched on the edge of a worn chair covered in dog hairs. *Sporting Life, Shooting Times, Horse and Hound* and *Country Life* spill from mahogany tables covered in water rings. In the grate the fire glows like a coffin lid on a cloudy day.

You meet your fellow guests, search gamely for common ground, and note with dismay that the most attractive girl in the room is the hostess's daughter.

In to dinner, to discover that the art of conversation is not lost, but totally extinct. A young man who tries to steer a general debate on the price of pony nuts into Third World politics is put down with, 'Well, of course, that's an old problem.' He will find that more 'old problems' surface as the weekend goes on, until he gives up. Drunken, incomprehensible game of bridge. Bed.

Saturday: You awake painfully at dawn, convinced you have been sleeping on the billiard-table. Vague sounds of animal life, both inside and out, permeate the room. Is that ominous snuffling outside the door something closing in for the kill, or the butler with chronic sinusitis?

You run a few inches of bathwater, cold enough to paralyse a polar bear, and dress hurriedly to keep warm. At breakfast fellow-guests sit numbed, or exhilarated, by similar experiences.

Land-Rovers and shooting brakes riddled with dry rot arrive. Everyone piles in for a day's hunting or shooting. The next six hours are spent struggling manfully to avoid a broken limb, or perforated eardrums (perhaps even both).

Later, you return to dress, aching, for dinner. As your collar stud rolls under the bed you stumble upon the remains of the last guest, who died from hypothermia. One of the lucky ones. An inexplicable pain surges from the top of your neck to your ankle.

Over dinner you make a half-hearted attempt at footsie with a girl from Christie's opposite, until your hostess's octogenarian father, next to her, starts choking on his Tarte Tatin. Drunken, incomprehensible charades. Bed.

Sunday: Brisk start, and much deep breathing, followed by heavy breakfast. Morning ride on hyperactive hunter. Quells. Alka Seltza. Lie down in darkened room to the distant crash of croquet mallets.

Lunch. Frenzied tennis with teenage family members who insist on shouting 'You're the *pits*'. They are replaced by energetic adults who call 'Sorry!', at thirty-second intervals.

You unsuccessfully attempt to grapple with a throbbing head by plunging into the pool. Wracked with instant cramp, you swoosh from sub-zero water like a Polaris missile.

Tea. Profuse thanks for a wonderful weekend. Drive home aching and unfulfilled to the welcome prospect of a week's well-earned rest at the office.

Travelling hopefully

The art of the flamboyant arrival is, sadly, all but forgotten. Ever since King Alfonso of Spain turned up for a week's grouse shooting in Scotland by battleship, things have gone steadily downhill.

Helicopters – before they were discovered by commodity brokers and chat-show hosts – cut something of a dash, but the rotary club are not noted for their good works in rural England. Blasting all the petals from your hostess's rose-bed, precipitating a mass stampede in the piggery and slicing through the telephone wires, all before you have even introduced yourself, do not auger well for a happy weekend. The ubiquitous chopper does have its compensations, however. It avoids rousing sleeping lodge-keepers to open the gates, and is splendid for dodging the breathalyser. At Christmas, Cotswold skies are black with weaving ironmongery, fuelled on Glüwein and G & T, looking for a place to roost.

On foot, negotiating even a short passage to your host's front door can be hazardous. Country estates are landmined with animal refuse which has a remarkable adhesive power to town shoes. Even worse is a certain castle in the South of England, which is completely surrounded by ancient animal traps of all descriptions – including several fully-primed man-traps. The hall is full of stuffed beasts which have fallen foul of the defences. No human

Blasting all the petals from your hostess's rose-bed as you arrive does not augur well for a happy weekend.

heads are mounted on the walls, but the few guests who accept invitations rarely venture outdoors.

A spate of Raffles-style break-ins has precipitated a boom in the guard-dog industry. Unwary guests run the increasing risk of being trapped in their cars, with the windows tightly closed, by zealous dobermans. It becomes a frantic race against time to attract your host's attention with blasts of the horn before the oxygen runs out. If all else fails, drive back to the gatehouse and telephone. Should the first signs of hyperventilation occur, engage first gear, drive up the steps and force open the front doors with the bumper.

Even safely indoors there is no escape from the attentions of inquisitive animals. A guest at Lady Clifford's was advised to leave his room only at pre-arranged times, when the dog was safely off-duty. At one famous house, guests are advised to lock their cars in an out-building resembling a disused aircraft hangar – erected to protect vehicles from some wandering goats with a penchant for car tyres.

Rugged transport is an obvious advantage for negotiating rutted drives. The approach to some homes is like a JCB test track. Without robust suspension, and a spade for digging yourself out of the mud, the weekend begins and ends at the gates. The rusting shells of abandoned sports cars give a clue to what lies ahead.

One of the few places where the throaty roar of a well-tuned engine rises like a consumptive lark on the morning air, is Basford Hall. Averil Scott-Moncrieff, and her husband Bunty, keep a Bugatti in the bedroom. A long, rocky slope leads from the first floor down to the drive. Mrs Scott-Moncrieff, a grandmother with a taste for speed, can be seen in leather helmet and goggles, roaring from the boudoir for a morning spin.

Pack up your troubles

People brought up in the country do little more than throw a threadbare Barbour, a spare Guernsey and battered brown suitcase into the back of the Golf GTi, and head for home. Those made of lesser stuff would be wise to play it safe and pack accordingly.

The overwhelming problem encountered in a country house is the wind chill factor. Victorian central-heating engineers had an all-or-nothing approach to their art. Their systems, still happily clanking in Heath-Robinson splendour, were not designed to be regulated; they have only two settings, and in most houses it is invariably 'Off'. The problem of what to wear in such circumstances can be further complicated if the family live in the kitchen, huddled round a struggling fire.

The bathrooms, in particular, of large, old country houses are as cosy as the Albert Hall, notoriously freezing, and invariably booby-trapped by Victorian plumbers. Guests who are already innured to the Wagnerian crescendoes of the water system can be paralysed by the arctic conditions, both in the bath and out of it.

Country-dwellers, on the other hand—raised on nightly duckings in freezing tubs from muscular nannies—are oblivious to the discomfort and alarming medical consequences. Rangey and red-cheeked, they thrive on spartan living. Lord Rokeby, for one, had a

The bathrooms, in particular, of large, old country houses are as cosy as the Albert Hall, notoriously freezing and booby-trapped by Victorian plumbers.

passion for cold water. Most of his eighty-eight years were spent floating cheerfully in icy baths. Weekend guests taking a brisk constitutional would be concerned to find him lying partially submerged in the garden pond.

I know one veteran house-guest who has kept a detailed record of the time it takes for hot water to splutter forth after the tap has been turned on. The fastest—logged with the aid of a stopwatch—is four minutes, forty seconds. The record: never.

Most houses have three or four bathrooms, and a hot-water system geared to supply a large dog's bowl. The first tepid issue is heralded by a loud banging of pipes, which shivering guests may understandably mistake for their hostess hammering on the door to see if they are still alive. And once the ordeal is over, a pair of stout running shoes will be needed for the sprint back to the faintly-glowing single-bar fire in the bedroom, which can be up to a quarter of a mile away.

Sadly, the salvo of ear-shattering spirit-rappings may not, in the end, be an indication that good news is coming through. Then, the only course left open is the standard thirty-second, country-house bath; followed by advanced hypothermia.

Scottish lodges, usually opened only for the red deer season, are frequently miles from the nearest mains supply. They rely on local hill water, which emerges from the taps in a rich, peat-brown trickle; a treat for anyone who enjoys taking a dip in ice-cold Darjeeling. Foil body blankets discarded from the London Marathon, and a nip of brandy, are the sensible answer.

Roddy Llewellyn recounts the cautionary tale of a weekend visit to a large country house, when his bedside glass of water froze solid. A regular guest at a gale-swept fortress perched above the Firth of Forth doggedly wears a fur coat throughout his visits, which is considered quite acceptable by his hosts. On the other hand, a guest elsewhere completely blew his credibility when it was discovered that he had removed several wooden slats supporting the mattress on his bed and used them, Colditz-style, to keep the anaemic bedroom fire burning. Thermal underwear would have been more discreet.

Norfolk's reputation is unequalled for the freezing temperatures of its old houses. The record-holder, now tagged and emptied by Christies, was Elveden, where the only chatter to be heard round the dinner-table was that of the guests' teeth. One marble-lined room, transformed into an arctic Taj Mahal by the Maharajah of the Punjab, is the size of a small cathedral and universally voted the coldest room in England.

Chic droppings

The rule of strict formality in informal country dress dictates that nothing should ever appear new.

There is an element of mystery here, as somewhere in Tyne and Wear, the Barbour factory is busy turning out new jackets by the thousand. Where they go is totally baffling, because new Barbours simply do not exist. For any kind of country cred, they must be threadbare, faded, crumpled and, preferably, flecked with tractor grease. The theory that they somehow improve with age is so widespread that, if someone ever held a Rotten Barbour Contest, half the population of rural England would tie for first place. The other half would be wearing equally decrepit Huskies.

Thereby lies an insight into the vicissitudes of those who have stoutly resisted anything new or foreign for centuries. How did the brainwave of an *American* air force colonel, Stephen Guylas, become part of the British way of life in just twenty years? Huskies have taken over Badminton Horse Trials like kiss-me-quick hats at Blackpool.

Fashion note: If you have to buy a new Barbour, do try to arrange to have it run over several times by tractor before appearing in public. The result will enable you to blend into the landscape without difficulty. Barbours with hoods are strictly for youth leaders and retired insurance managers from Brent Cross.

Things to absent-mindedly pull out of your Barbour pockets:
Old pony nuts

If you have to buy a new Barbour, do try to arrange to have it run over by a tractor before appearing in public. The result will enable you to blend into the landscape without difficulty.

A half-wrapped mint humbug covered in chaff
Baling twine
A folding hoof-pick
Tangled dog leads
A couple of cartridges
Dog-eared *Field* diary
Crumpled ticket from last year's Game Fair
Large, off-white linen handkerchief

Things never to pull out of your Barbour pockets:
False teeth
3-D key rings of Charles and Diana
Packet of ten Cadets
A folded copy of *Exchange and Mart*
Souvenir purses from Benidorm
Swiss Army knife
Contraceptives

When it comes to buying green wellies, there is only one acceptable type: Hunters. However, to be able to tell why they are better, you need a piano-tuner's ear. Hunters are superior because they resonate better. When slapped with a riding crop or walking stick they emit a commanding thwack, compared with the dull thud of lesser breeds. In addition, the little half-straps—seldom understood and never used—signal instantly that you do not have a day job at McAlpines.

When is a green wellie not a green wellie? When it's a gum boot, sprouting like intensively-farmed leeks at point-to-points, game fairs and in stable yards.

There presumably exists a vast black market in spray-on mud. Even in the hottest, earth-cracking summer, Hunters are streaked with the stuff. They shine not, neither do they squeak. Nor shall the tops thereof be down-turned—for the vengeance of the people shall be great.

People nurture their wellies and grow terribly fond of them, rather like pet rocks. However, rubber repair patches are impossible to obtain. There is not a single factory in Britain producing them—much to the annoyance of fly fishermen who continually snag green waders on barbed wire fences. They eccentrically attend to them with bicycle puncture outfits, which give the appearance of the walking Black Death. And when, like old soldiers, antique green wellies quietly fade away, they are replaced by another pair which looks even older. (The same rule of thumb extends to study furniture and tweed jackets.)

Mad dogs and Englishmen

One sure way to the heart of any host or hostess is to make engaging comments about their dogs. Working dogs flop beside brogues and hunting boots in family portraits, spend their lives depositing puddles on hall floors, and are laid to rest in their own little plot in the garden along with the rest of the domestic menagerie.

Platoons of labradors, spaniels, terriers, and whippets feign deafness and refuse to budge from fireside chairs, or trip up unsuspecting visitors and savage their Gucci bags like dead rats. Everyone, of course, blithely ignores them—except the parvenu who loathes dogs from the very bottom of his marrowbone jelly.

Dogs with the good fortune to have dotty owners completely take over a house. Compton Miller once told me of a house he was billeted at for a debs' dance, which was totally overrun by harlequin great danes. Four guests, feeling like lost refugees, were unable to find a square inch of chair or sofa which had not been claimed by a salivating beast. Their hostess, they discovered, bred vast packs of them. Any attempt to befriend one, and perhaps coax him onto the carpet, was thwarted by a piercing whistle. Instantly the doors flew open and the next shift burst in, tails thumping, to take their places.

Platoons of labradors, spaniels, terriers, and whippets trip up unsuspecting visitors and savage their Gucci bags like dead rats.

As relays of heavyweight harlequins thundered to and fro, the guests spent the evening crouched on the floor, covered in dog hairs. Efforts were made at strained conversation, but the hostess seemed totally unaware of their anguish.

But even those brought up in a lively atmosphere of rural idiosyncrasy can find dogs extremely unpredictable. A green wellie of my acquaintance returned to her bedroom during a house party to find the family's geriatric, half-blind labrador lying across her bed. A not-uncommon situation, but in its advancing years, the dog misinterpreted her friendly pat and sank the few teeth it had left into her arm. She managed to wrench herself free and made a stately, if dramatic descent to the dining-room—blood pumping down her evening dress in a scene of Hammer horror.

Country houses are notoriously devoid of any medical facilities for humans. Stiff Upper Lip requires one to bleed silently to death behind the Hepplewhite sofa (but never on it). On the other hand, cupboards are crammed with every conceivable brand of veterinary product; enough to service London Zoo several times over. The victim's hostess proceeded, with alacrity, to smear her with a foul green linament and strap her up with horse bandages, before resuming dinner as though nothing had happened.

Small creatures are rarely seen in country houses, except perhaps running along kitchen skirting boards. Cats are relegated to a working life in the stables, where they diligently eliminate most of the mouse population, and drive the rest to seek refuge in the house. There, safe in rooms where the dogs snooze all day, they can live in the style to which they are accustomed.

Inverary Castle is notably free of wee beasties. The Duke and Duchess of Argyll share their pannelled eighteenth-century dining-room with Bran, the family ferret. Unlike his brethren, who spend a bleak life winning bets in the uninviting confines of wallies' trousers, he drinks from a crystal goblet and has his whiskers lovingly dabbed with a linen napkin. Guests have been quite taken aback by their needle-toothed table companion.

The same reaction can be found at a beautiful Georgian house near Tain, Scotland (it must be the air up there), where bewildered

Cupboards are crammed with every conceivable brand of veterinary product; enough to service London Zoo several times over.

house-guests are confronted by a pet pig called Twiggy which trots around at dinner parties, crashing into the furniture.

However, back to dogs, and a story which I am convinced is one of those modern folk tales, like alligators in the New York sewers, and old ladies who glance in the rear-view mirror to find transvestite axemen in the back of the Beetle. It exudes so much anguish, that it must be rooted somewhere in the truth.

It concerns the hapless guest who sat down to dinner on a most uncomfortable chair. The more he wriggled and adjusted himself, the more lumpy and insufferable it became. Finally, he surreptitiously slid his hand beneath his bottom to discover that he had inadvertently suffocated his hostess's favourite chihuahua. Mortified with embarrassment he managed, between mouthfuls, to manoeuvre the lifeless creature inside his dinner jacket until he could decide how to dispose of it.

One can only suppose that he went on to be hauled reluctantly into a round of after-dinner charades, Moriarty, or Under the Blanket, still grimly hanging on to it.

Mongrels, with the exception of unkempt Jilly Cooper look-alikes, are less common in country houses, although the lurcher, a fast-rising Sloane favourite, has got his feet firmly under the mahogany table. In coursing they are far superior, in both brains and staying power, to greyhounds. And they give married couples a little gypsy mystique.

Whippets are beloved of both the well-heeled and the working classes. Country people love them because they find it hard to resist any great sporting dog, a weakness epitomized by the devoted followers of Smokey, the fastest whippet in England. His owner, a tinker called Murphy, made a handsome living plundering two adjoining estates in North Yorkshire, about twenty years ago, and by placing huge bets on Smokey's racing prowess. Landowners and coal miners alike had unsuccessfully matched their dogs against the emaciated rocket.

One day, Murphy was playing pontoon in his favourite Catterick local, when an immaculately-dressed stranger, who had motored the length of the country to make a wager, entered the bar. When he asked for Smokey's owner, the whole room suddenly fell silent. Murphy identified himself, and made his famous boast that his whippet could beat anything on four legs. They shook hands on a £1000 stake, the race to take place 300 miles away on a private estate near Welwyn.

The local gamekeeper chauffered Murphy, with Smokey beside them, in his Ford Popular—followed by a strange convoy of Bentleys and shooting-brakes from the local estates. The journey down the A1 took nine hours, allowing frequent halts for Smokey to hop out and relieve himself. When they arrived, a crowd of 1500 sporting people lined the 500 yd track, bubbling with anticipation. As enormous bets changed hands, Smokey was bundled into his trap, alongside his rival, who could be heard pawing impatiently for the Off.

Murphy positioned himself at the end of the track, swinging a dead rabbit taken at dawn that day. Next to him, the stranger lounged confidently, one hand thrust in his covert coat, the other holding a large Havanna cigar. When the traps crashed open, Smokey took off like a bullet—followed by an extremely large four-year-old cheetah. By a stroke of good fortune, the length of the track was less than the beast needed to reach its maximum speed and Smokey, hungry for the rabbit, won by a nose.

The Yorkshire estate-owners vied loudly to buy England's fastest whippet on the spot, but Murphy politely demurred. 'I couldn't sell me bread and butter now, could I, gentlemen?' he said.

Will that be all, sir?

Staff are a singular breed, either mute and long-suffering, or endowed with a sparkling talent for joining the mayhem when the occasion demands. One butler, of Continental extraction, is an accomplished tap-dancer, who can sashay into a soft shoe shuffle at the drop of a napkin.

Others show great forbearance – like the head butler at a famous Scottish house which became a bolt-hole for a former prime minister. As the PM spent every available hour in the river fly fishing, the butler had to take communications of State down to the waterside on a silver tray, roll up his trousers and wade in to deliver them. Three out of four would be skimmed downstream in case they necessitated a hasty return to London.

Behind the impassive face of every butler lurks an air of unmistakable superiority. These days he is, after all, the man most likely to unpack your suitcase and arrange its contents – however personal. Short of wiring the handle with a high-voltage coil, the guest is completely at the mercy of his knowing look. Someone, somewhere – and he knows who – is still cringing with embarrassment at the discovery of a bull whip and a nurse's uniform laid out neatly on his bed.

The few Baroque butlers left in service have a habit of dog-earing

Staff are a singular breed.

a visiting card, thus cracking the ivory patina and preventing its re-use by impostors. Irritating if it happens to be the only calling card you possess.

Rogue butlers are surprisingly rare. One or two have had their patience tried beyond endurance and run amok with 12-bores, but amazingly most of them manage to keep their feelings to themselves.

An engaging exception was Tivendale, who made a modest, if bizarre, living leaving a trail of hysteria in dozens of country houses. He would take up a new appointment and, for some plausible reason, obtain a month's salary in advance. Two or three days after his arrival there would invariably be a formal dinner party. Tivendale would glide solicitously into the dining-room with a soup tureen and solemnly tip it between the neck and collar of the nearest guest.

He was, of course, sacked immediately. No charges were pressed because of the embarrassment involved, leaving the gentleman of soup-stance free to move on to repeat his routine elsewhere. He eventually found himself well and truly in the Muligatawny when he was arrested for writing his own references.

The traditional advice given to trainee butlers is: 'Don't ever take a drink – they *always* think you've been at theirs.'

Suspicion led to drastic measures at a house in Berkshire when the titled owner, retiring to bed, noticed that the sherry was half an inch lower in the decanter. He carefully marked the level and found, to his astonishment, that it had dropped again the following evening. By a process of elimination the blame fell on the butler. Over the next few days the sherry continued to recede until, simmering like a corked volcano, he decided to take action. The gentleman placed the decanter on the floor, unbuttoned his trousers and topped it up. He was somewhat stunned to notice that the level continued to fall by the same amount each day.

Unable to suppress his anger, he cornered the butler and demanded to know if he had been responsible. The man confessed without hesitation.

'If you recall, sir,' he said, 'the doctor advised you to have a tablespoonful in your soup each day.'

How to address a butler
My dear fellow
By his surname
By ignoring him completely

How not to address a butler
Mate
John
Squire
Sir

Running with the pack

A weekend guest may occasionally realize, to the well-concealed mirth of the family, that the horse he or she has been allocated for a day's hunting is perhaps not as somnambulistic as it was made out to be. And hacking to the meet on a four-legged Exocet can be a nerve-racking experience for the novice. Especially when, in some remote lane, a muck-spreader driver nursing a hangover decides to challenge for right-of-way.

As with most things in hunting there is a rule of thumb. Highway etiquette consists of: reining-in with a courteous nod for Bentleys, Land-Rovers and ancient shooting-brakes; forcing all Fords, Vauxhalls, sports cars and anything Japanese into the most convenient ditch; and trampling Reliant Robins outright.

Down the centuries, hunting has acquired distinct military overtones, with an emphasis on correct turn-out and a willingness to risk appalling injury for baffling objectives. The uninitiated find it a minefield of social disaster, rather like bidding at Sotheby's art sales with an involuntary twitch. One false gesture, or a word out of place, can throw the whole event into total disarray.

Round-the-world yachtsman Chay Blyth learned this quickly on his first outing with his local hunt. He cheerily raised his hat and waved to the Master, unaware that it was a signal meaning: 'The fox is over here.' Fifty riders immediately wheeled their horses and thundered towards him in total confusion.

Cubbing, the prelude to the hunting season, begins during September, once the harvest is in. During the cubbing season young hounds learn how to give chase, young foxes learn how to escape from them, and young riders are 'blooded'.

The latter is a quaint ceremony which obsesses anti's and anthropologists alike. Lumps of freshly-killed meat are daubed on young faces in a strange initiation, peculiar only to the upper classes and certain tribes in New Guinea unreached by missionaries. Tradition dictates that the bloodstain should be worn proudly until the end of the day – not that Robin and Nicky would dream of allowing the au pair to clean it off anyway.

After cubbing, the hunting season proper runs from November to April, tailing-off into a vapour trail of balls, point-to-points and puppy shows. Then, before the leg is barely out of plaster, it's back in the saddle again.

Old hands regard themselves as 'fundamental people', wary of the waves of newcomers to the hunting field threatening to erode retreating standards. Although why anyone should worry is a mystery. One look at sneezing, aching weekenders limping back to their Range Rovers is enough to confirm that fundamental people are made from sterner stuff. It takes years of training to become impervious to the elements, long hours in the saddle and the rigours of pink gin.

The inexperienced would be well advised always to keep their horses facing the hounds. This way, there will be no danger of their kicking one. And during the chase they should keep at the tail of the field.

Those anxious to be seen, on the other hand, try desperately to keep up with the leaders, and thereby commit the cardinal sin of hunting. Always remember that it is unforgivable to override the huntsman. 'Thrusters' ruin the chance of catching Charlie by pushing the hounds and confusing the line. Offenders face a life sentence of sideways looks at social gatherings.

Nothing quite beats the romance of the Quorn (never on a cob)

It is unforgivable to override the huntsman.

and the Belvoir—rubbing shoulders with one's own kind, and perhaps raising a cap to HRH. Himself, incidentally, is rarely seen at stirrup-cup, preferring to break cover discreetly and join the field later. Theoretically, it puts press photographers off the scent, but as he is followed closely by his minder in a whining Land-Rover, wheels slipping furiously, much of the strategy is wasted.

For mere dumb beasts, horses owned by fundamental people have a commendable sense of social awareness. They may, for example, display an unequivocal aversion to family saloons under 1500 cc. Even a silently purring engine of the wrong marque has been known to have a moving effect on their internal combustion.

Horse manure may be highly prized by elderly village gardeners who follow the hunt with a bucket and shovel. And a discreet fleck or two is quite acceptable on mahogany-topped boots. But gallons running down the gleaming door panel of a Ford Sierra can be alarmingly corrosive.

The car's owner is presented with a testing moment. Should he: (a) risk certain exclusion by claiming on his third party insurance; (b) blot his copybook for all time by scrubbing it off, while sobbing quietly; or (c) mount up with a tight smile and make a mental note to chisel it away later? Happily there were never such problems in Surtees' day.

There are further reasons why those who box to a meet should be wary where they park. Horses enjoy hunting as much as their owners and become disturbingly frisky at the prospect of a run. Never assume that your essential accessories are safe. Horses with red tail ribbons are kickers and, unless you know a good panel-beater, should be given a wide berth.

The mere sight of the Master glancing at his pocket-watch threw an ageing, feeble-minded hunter into such paroxysms of joy at a Bodmin meet that he mistook a wholesale butcher's red Jaguar for the first hedge of the day. The horse, a heavyweight by any standards, leapt exuberantly into the air and reduced the bonnet to tenderized sirloin.

Dress must pass the critical eye of the Master. A white stock should be worn, wound tightly round the neck and secured by a

Nothing quite beats the romance of the Quorn and the Belvoir—rubbing shoulders with one's own kind and perhaps raising a cap to HRH.

plain gold pin (never one decorated with horse-shoes or horses' heads or, worse still, both), with loose ends held neatly down. The stock serves two purposes. It lessens the effect of whiplash injuries (inflicted by falls, not disapproving huntspeople), and is marvellous for holding broken necks in place long enough to force down a farewell brandy.

Those brought up to it have no difficulty in fixing their stock pins in the correct, horizontal position. Others should practise this, as a stock pin jabbed in vertically will result in a forcible tracheotomy at every jump.

Top hat, bowler or hunting cap and black coat are crucial—red is worn only at the Master's invitation—along with a Melton waistcoat backed in the same warm material. It is not worth scrimping by buying the cheap version with just a Melton front, as the resulting crab-like walk from a chapped bottom is a giveaway. A ratcatcher, incidentally, is not a frequent caller at old country houses, but a hacking jacket worn by children for cubbing.

Your breeches should be buff, worn with black boots, or white, worn with black boots with mahogany tops. Mixing the order is social death; even colour-blindness is not accepted as a mitigating factor. Flies are buttoned—nylon zips which burst open at the first fence are viewed with disapproval, by male members at least.

A titled veteran of the Zetland, fond of an *aprés*-hunt tincture, would telephone his groom to drive out to the pub with oats and bran for his tethered horse. Then, at 2 am, he would weave unsteadily through the village and blow his hunting-horn for the gamekeeper to follow him to the house to lever him out of his breeches. 'Confounded nuisance, these buttons,' he used to snort.

They can be stubborn, too, when peeing alfresco on a cold day. One of our best-known hunting Dukes was caught in the act of struggling to stow his family jewels, by a lady rider. Blushing furiously, she pretended not to notice. Unabashed he called: 'Have a good look, m'dear gel. There aren't many of these left in the country.'

Hunting crops, carried upside down by arrivistes, are raised primarily to thank motorists. They can also be used to spur on

Horses enjoy hunting as much as their owners do and become disturbingly frisky at the prospect of a run.

sluggish horses. Some are fitted with wrist straps to reduce the huge influx of newcomers to the sport. Only an idiot would use them and risk breaking a wrist in a fall.

An octogenarian huntsman has his crops specially made by Swaine, Adeney, Brigg who mount an eyeglass to the stock so that he can take aim before jumping.

However, looking the part is only half the battle. Apart from the obvious problems of staying in the saddle, a variety of less common skills may be called upon.

In the nether reaches of Britain, huntspeople are a rough-hewn bunch, ignorant of the nuances of stockbroker meets. The East Cornwall, in hot pursuit across the moor, came across a cow owned by one of the members. The beast was clearly on the point of calving, so the field dismounted, delivered the new arrival, and promptly galloped off again ...

Yurt, yurt, yurt

Hunting, like computing, has a strange language all of its own. It is not, however, user-friendly and social interface may be difficult.

An estimated six out of ten huntspeople nowadays are women, and inevitably there are a few MFHs among them. However, they should never be called the hunt-mistress, even if the stories you hear about their private lives indicate otherwise.

A vital cry to remember is 'ware wire'—bellowed when the field is heading for barbed wire. The correct pronunciation is 'wor wire'. When roared in a Birmingham accent by businessmen hunting in the Midlands, it can be interpreted as a speech impediment.

Dogs are creatures which cock their legs on the wrought iron gates of suburban homes called Dunroamin. Hounds, pronounced 'hinds' (which must be misleading when deerhunting) do not have tails, but sterns (starns). Instead of barking, like the rest of the canine *hoi polloi*, they 'give tongue'. Collectively, this is known as 'music', though weary locals may have another word for it.

When hounds have lost the line (i.e., scent), the whipper-in may occasionally be seen whispering encouragement into a silken ear or two. The correct form of address—should you ever be at a loss for conversation with a hound—is 'yurt, yurt, yurt'.

Assuming they know what you are yurting about, do they ever listen? In a day best forgotten by the Tickham, the pack moved off from Faversham railway station for a nearby covert.

Off they went, loyally loping after Charlie—and that was the last anyone saw of them. The whole pack, consisting of fifteen and a half couples (thirty-one hounds) disappeared for more than three hours, leaving the field in the unprecedented position of hunting for hounds instead of foxes. An embarrassed MFH had to summon the assistance of the local constabulary, who drafted in men to join the search. As dusk fell over Kent the hounds were discovered by a farmer three miles away trying to pick up a line on the whipper-in. Charlie was no doubt tucked up in bed laughing quietly.

Hounds are usually quite single-minded when working for a living, and whither they go, the field has to follow. One fox, objecting to excessive harassment, took the matter to his local MP. He leapt through the open dining-room window of the former member for North Bucks, followed by the entire hysterical pack of the Grafton. In a scene of total horror and pandemonium, it was finally dispatched beneath the dining-room table. The incident was thereafter presumably referred to as 'an old problem'.

Meat and drink

Hunting may not be, as Oscar Wilde said, 'the unspeakable in pursuit of the uneatable', but it has certainly left many a seasoned horseman speechless with indigestion. Thermos flasks, Tupperware containers and miners' snap-tins—the lunch-pack currency of the populace—are unheard of in the field. So how do stalwarts of the saddle sustain themselves? Surreptitiously, of course.

Those who are fearful of twenty miles boneshaking on an empty stomach, have been known to slip a Fortnum's paté sandwich into the pocket of their hunting jacket. However, voracious eaters tempted to take two are instantly rumbled by the suspicious bulge. Mars bars, for obvious reasons, are out. So is cheese—too crumbly;

The correct form of address —should you ever be at a loss for conversation with a hound —is
'yurt, yurt, yurt'.

and roast ham – prone to flying from the bread and laying a false line when whipped hastily from the pocket. Pickles? Well, there was the embarrassed horseman whose attention was frostily drawn to a rapidly-spreading brown stain on his flank.

At a Norfolk meet, which shall remain nameless, three hunts-people, fearful of the disapproval of the Master, detached themselves one by one from the field and slipped into a copse, where they munched away. Each believed he was unobserved. At a sudden noise they looked up simultaneously to discover – not only each other – but the Master himself scoffing away behind a tree.

Drink is a more acceptable problem. The hunting day begins with stirrup cup shortly before eleven, with a pause for chasing Charlie, before resuming at the nearest hostelry. Hip flasks are pocketed discreetly, unlike in Jorrocks' day when horsemen openly slung generous containers from the saddle for fortification. A nip of the right stuff could keep a flagging rider going all day. One flushed huntsman of 100 years ago waxed: 'My spirit rushed before me as I felt the '34 percolating through my system – noble vintage, now no more.'

He, like those who have followed, had to contend with the major drawback of life in the hunting saddle: miles of rolling, lavatory-less landscape. Robust drinkers – indeed anyone with a weak bladder – should think twice before aspiring to hunt membership.

There is the cautionary tale of an attractive friend who was taken short on open moorland, mercifully in thick fog. She discreetly checked that the coast was clear before resorting to what is known colloquially as the 'huntsman's squat'. She was crouched beside her patient mount, when the entire East Cornwall loomed from the mist at a leisurely walk. As they filed past each member respectfully raised his cap . . .

Injuries, various

The great dilemma of those new to hunting is whether to arrive correctly turned-out in top hat or bowler – and run the not unlikely risk of spending the rest of their lives as vegetables – or to opt for the sensible precaution of a crash-helmet and chinstrap. These add an undeniable dash to the couture of point-to-point riders and foreign riot police, but in the strict etiquette of the hunting field they are still considered a little nouveau. Concern for bodily safety is not an attribute to be displayed openly.

Fundamental people stoically haul around pounds of internal ironmongery; pins hold legs together, jaws are wired-up, and it is rumoured that there is even the odd bolt in the neck (ideal for social scoring at airport metal-detectors on the way to Longchamps). Surgical appliances may lack a certain *élan* but, worn correctly, imbue the sufferer with a desirable air of long experience in the saddle. In the best houses everyone creaks down to breakfast; the Marquess of Hertford's entire family once spent Christmas in plaster casts. Nevertheless despite their frequency and severity, hunting injuries should be borne philosophically; they should never be allowed to become a topic of conversation for more than thirty seconds. Fundamental people have mastered the art of putting the casual into casualty.

There is a certain timeless quality about the clatter of colliding crutches at the hunt ball. On a fashion note, women with broken arms and collar bones should always seek the support of a Hermes scarf (horse motif optional). For men, regulation hospital calico is *de rigeur*.

Faced with the ever-present threat of hospitalization after falling in some corner of a foreign field, it is wise to pull on clean underwear from Turnbull and Asser before a meet. Accidents should be suffered with a polite rejection of help, and a degree of obstinacy increasing with age. Many an old buffer has been seen fighting stretcher-bearers all the way to the Land-Rover. Novices can score heavily by ignoring injuries–though a rueful grin of apology may be permissible while wrestling one's shoulder back into its socket. Happily, however, the field is seldom short of a doctor or two; extraordinary men who execute complex first aid procedures while keeping one eye firmly fixed on the hounds.

Concussives have a reputation for remounting. This is an ill-advised move, as the effects can often be delayed. The MFH of one of the oldest hunts in the country was retiring to bed at 1 am after an energetic day, when there was a thundering on the front door. He opened it to find a prominent member, still in hunting dress, holding the bridle of his exhausted horse and demanding to know why everyone had gone home.

Fundamental people appear to have little regard for cranial safety. It has been unkindly said that this, after all, is the least vulnerable part of their anatomy. Huntsmen and committee members sail over stone walls with little more than a velvet cap for protection – followed by a cautious assortment of riders worrying about their cosmetic dentistry. They are a familiar sight at the first wide ditch, on hands and knees in the mud, searching for crowns and contact lenses. Hunt followers without the benefit of field-glasses have mistaken them for hounds trying frantically to pick up the line.

One can only wonder how permanent the damage from falls on the head might be. Lord Willoughby used to recall the story of a friend who, after a long day with the Warwickshire, was convinced he had been out with the Cottesmore.

There is a discredited theory that cranial thickness increases correspondingly with family line. It was perhaps prompted by a fearless huntsman of the 1890s, called John Jones, who actually loved falling off his horse. After picking himself up once again from the mud, he shouted excitedly to a novice: 'Fifty minutes and seven falls, my boy! Not bad for an old 'un.'

In the pink

In the heady abandon of the hunt ball triumphs are relived and, occasionally, old grievances surface to enliven the evening. Not that many hunt balls need enlivening. Bawdy fancy dress competitions, bun fights and groping under tables are not unknown.

Drink has a habit of getting the better of some guests. At an Oxfordshire shindig, a young farmer, built like a combine harvester, decided to take it out on a quiet, diminutive newcomer whose hunting reputation was less than adventurous. Members smirked behind gin glasses when the farmer began to shove him around, but he refused to rise to the challenge.

Finally, goaded beyond endurance, he leapt six feet into the air, with an ear-splitting scream, and felled the drunk with a well-aimed kick from his patent leather evening shoe. The silence was deafening. Some people really just don't know how to be fundamental . . .

Encounters with a horseless carriage

On at least one occasion the horseless carriage has unintentionally ridden to hounds. In an incident of excruciating embarrassment a yellow van hired by thirty hunt saboteurs beat the East Lincolnshire Hare Hounds to the kill.

They assembled near Skegness, in a cluster of anoraks and military surplus, to block the path of the approaching horsemen and hounds. The hare, going at full stretch, suddenly accelerated into view and was struck by the van.

As the Master hastened to put it out of its misery, the driver is reported to have snatched it up and bashed its head on the road.

'It's ironic, isn't it,' said the Master, Giles Crust. 'Here was me thinking you'd come to save wildlife.'

According to observers, the sab at this point went berserk. 'The blood of this animal is on your head,' he shouted, incensed. Whereupon he clubbed Master Crust over the head with it, leapt into his van and roared away.

The life and death of
the party

Green Wellie dinner parties are fertile ground for match-making mothers searching for a mate for Amanda–plump, and at a loose end since the porcelain restoration course ended. (Amanda, high on porcelain cement, is living happily with a guitarist she picked up at the Freedom Ball.)

Mothers apply themselves energetically to the occasion, flinging themselves headlong across the sofa during charades ('*Superwoman*, darling! I thought you'd never guess').

Fathers, on the other hand, make deep grumbling noises and stay out of the way as much as possible. One newly-arrived young man was sitting in a comfortable chair by the drawing-room fire, waiting for the other guests to come downstairs. Suddenly his host came striding into the room, and he hastily stood up: 'I hope I wasn't sitting in your chair?'

'They're *all* my chairs,' his host rumbled.

The full extent of a besieged father's conversation is a gruff: 'How d'ar do', followed by a brief salvo of abruptly barked questions:

> 'Work in the City?'
> 'Come down here often?'
> 'So, you're one of the Price-Twytts, eh?'

If the youth pinned against the Sheraton secretaire, sherry trembling, can slip in an 'Absolutely', or 'In no way', he passes muster.

As age erodes the faculties, conversations between the same generation become more telegraphic:

> 'Man's an arsehole . . .'
> 'Really . . . One of the Berkshire Arseholes?'

Silence understandably descends upon a sea of new faces from time to time. However, attempts to fill the void with hasty comments on the family portraits can have the same effect as tossing a hand grenade into a cess-pit. The ugly old buffer glaring down on everyone with a wart on his nose may turn out to be the hostess's mother. Some family portraits, far from providing diversions, have a knack of creating dumbfounded silence themselves. A recent painting of Lord Hertford's family at Ragley Hall has the unmistakable outline of a UFO floating above the noble assembly of heads. It was featured because a relative, Lady Jardine, is a member of the Atherius Society, whose members believe that flying saucers are commuting to earth to intercede for us.

According to the plethora of party books, the perfect bash must have the right balance of guests. In reality, a well-run dinner party, with its ping-pong of polite table talk, is as much fun as waking up with a dead policeman. Bernard Shaw, who attended more than his quota, once tartly admitted: 'I enjoyed myself because there was nothing else to enjoy.'

Country house dinner parties are the splendid exception; they are a cocktail of braying Henries, dribbling dogs helping themselves to smoked salmon, elderly relatives drifting through the room, deaf as adders, and stoic mothers swanning bravely through the confusion. Anywhere but England it could only end in group therapy or mass arrest.

Eccentric hosts add an invigorating air of the unexpected. Osborne de Vere, the late Duke of St Albans and a stickler for punctuality, would become visibly impatient when his wife took a long time to dress for dinner. After glancing irritably at his watch, he once offered her seat to a workman who had come to refill the fire extinguishers. The Duchess was obliged to eat in the kitchen, while the bewildered man struggled gamely with her meal.

Debrett on dinner parties has all the spontaneity of a state funeral. Are there *really* people, outside gay gatherings, who open conversations with: 'If you were the Queen, what opera/ballet/play would you choose to be performed for your Gala?' Beware too, of those who employ another Debrett opening gambit: 'I'm so glad you've come to live at Munstead Parva. We always thought that your house was the prettiest in the village.' They know that either it's riddled with dry rot, or something unspeakable was once exhumed from beneath the floorboards. Then there is the fatal: 'What is the nicest thing that happened to you today?' In reply to which I long to hear: 'Reversing repeatedly over your dachshund, actually.'

All this, of course, presupposes that conversation is possible. There is a very ugly Edwardian house in Hampshire with enormous stained-glass windows, and a vaulted sitting-room the size of an average church. Guests have to shout at each other in order to be heard, and any conversation is totally lost in a reverberating echo.

Thank heavens, then, for the great British hollow-legged, horse-slapping, ash-dropping country hostess, in her ancient tweed skirt and Husky which can probably be removed only by surgery. A fine example of the genre is a lady of distinguished lineage who inhabits a howling Victorian castle bearing all the hallmarks of the individualist. Nancy Mitford's U and Non-U have absolutely no meaning for those who have disappeared down the social U-bend. Chateau Naff has plastic dolls hanging from the chandeliers, and a large branch housing half a dozen obsolete wasps' nests propped in the corner, obscuring the rococo plasterwork.

The fraught tedium of polite dinner talk is unknown in her company. During one memorable dinner party an unfortunate girl from the kitchen tripped over a sleeping labrador, sending a large silver tray of cut melon crashing to the floor. The hostess ordered all the guests to pick up the pieces, and scrape the dog hairs from each one.

The grouse, which could have been appreciated only by a volleyball team, was served with a mountain of mashed potato buried under enough parsley to camouflage a Chieftain tank. As the butler solemnly held a silver basin brimming with the creamy concoction at her elbow, she scooped up a spoonful, held it high above her head, and let it splatter on to her plate.

'Cowpats!' she bellowed gleefully. 'We're having cowpats!'

More high-level bombings followed, leaving guests looking like the victims of an explosion in a wallpaper-paste factory.

The 'highlight' of the evening—a deb dance at a house a few miles away—was anticipated with light relief. A convoy of cars set off, tail-lights rising and falling on the mile-long, pot-holed drive, as the doomed guests followed their enthusiastic hostess in her purple Rolls.

Three hours later their worst fears were realized. Her aim with mashed potato was equalled by her skill at navigation. She hung a sudden right and the party juddered to a halt in the middle of a very dark, frozen field.

Parties at Chateau Naff are surpassed only by those once held at Antrim Castle. The Earl of Masserene—the appropriately-named Clotworthy Skeffington—had a passion for dining alfresco. To the despair of long-suffering guests, the mood would often take him in the middle of dinner. Perspiring staff would have to manhandle the heavy table and chairs through the window, and hoist them by block and tackle to the roof. Guests, wracked with indigestion, would toil upstairs for the next course. Then, as a forkful of Lobster Thermidor was halfway to an expectant mouth, the Earl would sniff the air—and order the whole lot downstairs again.

Home-killed game is traditional fare when country-weekending. However, nowadays an increasing number of impoverished hosts offer vegetarian good-life meals of home-grown produce. It is difficult to refuse steaming mounds of broccoli and French beans (aptly known as Jersey Runners), from proud

The Earl of Masserene had a passion for dining alfresco.

couples who have toiled long and hard to wrest them from the kitchen-garden.

Unfortunately, five courses of fresh compost can play havoc with the internal combustion. Thunderous involuntary reports tend to richochet round the dinner-table towards the end of the self-sufficient dinner. When the beans take their toll, the correct technique is never to admit responsibility. Instead, turn in mild surprise and cock an eyebrow at the person sitting next to you. Your hosts, inured to earthy, staccato interruptions, will continue unabashed, perhaps adding the occasional modest contribution themselves. This is a ripe time to turn the conversation to vegetables. Compliment them on the richness of their Meteors and Bedfordshire Champions.

Help me make it through the night

The last guest falls upstairs in a haze of Dows 45 – or any port in a storm – and the house grows quiet. Then, at about 3 am, comes the moment of reckoning, when, disorientated and desperate, you try frantically to recall your hostess's directions to the bathroom. It is one of those sobering moments in life when every door looks identical, and the slightest creak can surround the unwary with baying mastiffs.

One guest of my acquaintance, fearful of walking into someone else's bedroom, remembered in a flash of inspiration a large rosebush outside the drawing-room window. He crept downstairs, somehow managed to negotiate an array of front-door locks which would have done justice to Coutts, and stealthily padded outdoors in his pyjamas. Just as blessed relief suffused him, he somehow triggered off a burglar alarm, which bathed the grounds in floodlights and sent bells ringing all the way to the village police station. Rigid with terror, he was confronted by the entire household, in night attire, headed by his host clutching a 12-bore.

Even an encyclopaedic memory of the layout of the house is no guarantee of safe conduct. The master plumbers who installed the waterworks of country houses vied with each other for ingenuity, leaving a legacy of complex systems which have baffled generations of users.

It is one of those sobering moments in life when every door looks identical, and the slightest creak can surround the unwary with baying mastiffs.

In Scotland, for instance, one Victorian house has a large brass crank for flushing the lavatory, which must be rotated then reversed a precise number of degrees to operate. The careless face the excruciating consequence of the antique bowl flushing loudly and continuously throughout the night.

One English Duke has a metal plaque beneath his high, cast-iron cistern. Dated 1880, it warns users to protect themselves from an unexpected downpour. More than a century later, shocked guests still return to the drawing-room in soaking dinner-jackets, and hair plastered to their faces.

Trigger happy

They shall not pass

Huntsmen can blame a bad day on Charlie ... anglers are old hands at blaming just about anything ... bad shots, however, have no excuse. They are rare among those bred to the task, but if you did not serve a childhood apprenticeship carrying father's cartridge bag, and forcibly chanting Commander Mark Beaufoy's 'Never, never let your gun ...', the only decent thing to do is hastily enrol at a shooting school. Otherwise, on some lonely moor, you may die from exposure – of the social variety.

To shoot your host is quite unforgivable. As one old landowner put it: 'Getting hit is painful, whoever pulls the trigger – but it's more galling to be peppered by a bad shot than a good one.'

There is an often-told story about the Duke of Devonshire, who managed to kill a wounded pheasant – along with the retriever pursuing it. The dog's owner fell, wounded in the leg, together with the chef who was standing on the sidelines. The Duke hurried over, tortured with anxiety, to enquire how serious the chef's injuries were. After all, dinner might well have been ruined.

In the old days, beaters would be bagged with monotonous regularity. Geriatric gamekeepers can roll up their sleeves and trouser-legs and offer a guided anatomical tour of memorable shooting seasons. As the new generation are more disposed to litigation than forelock-tugging, a well-stuffed wallet or comprehensive insurance is advisable.

How unlike yesteryear, when Lord Cardigan cornered his head keeper and asked why the beaters were all men, when young lads could be hired at half the rate.

'Your Lordship may remember,' he replied, 'that last year you shot down all the boys ...'

There is, of course, the old philosophy that if you manage to hit anything, it can be regarded as sport. The only time this has proved true was in 1886 when William O'Malley, MP for Connemara, let rip at a grouse and missed. The shot passed straight through a hare and killed a 10 lb salmon in mid-leap on the river nearby.

Making the party go with a bang

Anyone contemplating a day's shooting is advised to invest in the right equipment: obligatory Barbour, and studded Hunter boots or, if you can't afford them, waterproof leggings to hide your Polyveldts. A brown Derby and plus-fours go a long way towards a future invitation. Designer skeet jerkins and army surplus jackets guarantee that you'll never get another.

Real Shooting People carry their cartridges in monogrammed pigskin bags, though two-gun shoots of the type enjoyed by the Duke of Westminster, HRH, Lord Litchfield and Prince Andrew, have a reputation for going through ammunition by the container-load. *Shooting Times* describes these days as 'megabags' – in excess of 1000 brace a day. But, unless you have a matched pair of Purdeys (the cheapest leave little change out of £20,000) feign illness.

Most enthusiastic shoots sound like the Western Front all over again, so the most vital piece of kit is a box of paracetamol, preferably the largest your Barbour pocket will accommodate. If challenged, remind your host that Lord Bertie Vane-Tempest–shooting's answer to Bugsy Malone–used to suffer stiff necks and splitting headaches too.

Dogs may be taken by invitation, but only if they are an acceptable breed and properly trained. You may have adored Dolores ever since you found her in Battersea Dogs' Home, but if she bolts up your breeks at the first salvo she will not be popular. Even less so, if she happens to be on heat and offers herself to every retriever in sight. There *are* easier ways to get yourself a well-bred gun-dog.

The wisest approach is to avoid anything on four legs. One of Willie Whitelaw's daughters was once asked to hold a pair of Irish wolfhounds which, she was assured, were gun-trained. When the first drive opened like an anti-aircraft battery, they took off—dragging her through a gorse bush.

In the normal course of events, the guns draw for their position in the first drive, and positions are rotated after each drive. A host will say 'up two' or 'down two', and the guns shuffle accordingly. Americans unfamiliar to grouse shooting look stunned when invited to take their butt . . . convinced they are being asked to leave.

Beaters are fond of driving towards the line shouting 'Brr brr brr'. Novices should note that this does not indicate that they are feeling the cold. Some prefer to call 'Hi hi, hi hi, hi hi'—to which at least one bemused American businessman has waved back and replied: 'Hi fellas.'

As the birds rise the rustic tribal cries change dramatically to shouts of 'Cock up!' For the sake of propriety this should never be interpreted as an instruction. 'Cock left' or 'Cock right' may quickly follow. Most townies use the phrase only in conversation with their tailor. In the field it simply means drop your hip flask and shoot.

After a liquid lunch the beaters' vocabulary becomes riper, especially if the bag leaves a lot to be desired. They are by nature an unruly bunch, disciplined only by the prospect of a tip.

One retired military gentleman, determined to knock some shape into his straggling platoon, resorted to a bizarre strategy. Each man was issued with a kind of over-vest, bearing a different letter of the alphabet, so that his progress through the covert could be monitored.

The beaters, scarcely concealing their annoyance, bore the indignity all morning. However, during the first drive after lunch, the guests were confronted by a line of men who had arranged themselves to spell out what they thought of the idea, in no uncertain terms.

Ruffled feathers

Pheasant have the grace to rise, flapping wildly, like early flying-machines, which at least allows time for snatches of conversation. Grouse tend to come in low and fast, twisting like a contour-hugging missile. It is considered more sporting to take high birds, but a corkscrewing grouse often tempts low shots. Proceed with caution: those grouse beaters, driving slowly across the moor waving white flags, may be signalling surrender.

The ultimate in bad form is to shoot your neighbour's bird. But if he has already loosed two barrels, and you hear him cursing, then you may smugly bring the bird down. In shooting circles this is known as 'wiping his eye'.

Elderly guns, not gifted with remarkable memory, should never be underestimated. At the end of a drive each will claim total recall of where his birds have landed.

Often, someone on the adjoining stand takes exception, and the familiar cries of '*My* bird, I think!' shatter the mellow peace of a December morning. Forget any subtle ploys to increase your bag by offering: 'Your bird, I think . . .' They fail miserably. Shooting is full of unmitigated bounders who retort, 'Absolutely old man'—when they know full well it isn't.

A monumental argument of Basil Fawlty proportions once erupted on Lord Ripon's estate. As he cautiously approached to investigate, he discovered one guest pelting his neighbour with dead grouse, and shouting in vibrant disgust: 'Here, take the damn lot! See if I care—take the lot, damn you!'

When the situation is clearly getting out of hand, the intervention of a third party often helps to diffuse matters. Two guns on a Scottish moor were almost coming to blows over a dead bird lying in no-man's-land–until the rightful owner's loader gently tugged his jacket tail. 'Let him have it, sir,' he whispered. 'I've got *two* of his.'

If word reaches you that the party will have army officers in its ranks, accept eagerly. There is a nasty rumour that they are surprisingly poor shots–rifle-trained on sitting targets, and appallingly ham-fisted with a 12-bore on feathered tornadoes.

There is probably an element of truth in the slander. A former gamekeeper, on 2000 acres of MOD property, claims that he was frequently called upon to uphold the good name of the Service. After a shoot he would be discreetly asked to put a brace of pheasant in the boot of each staff car. To ensure that there was enough to send them all home with, he would have to rise at dawn and bag them himself.

One notable exception is the Duke of Kent, renowned for standing knee-deep in personal megabags. On a Yorkshire estate the birds rose, almost by divine hand, to fly in droves over his peg alone. One guest, safely out of earshot, was heard to grumble: 'They must know he's a Royal–they've laid on a bloody fly-past.'

Pheasant country can, by nature, be quite dense, and when walked-up guns are in unfamiliar territory there is no knowing what may lie around the next corner. At an informal weekend shoot, a pheasant landed on the roof of a nearby gardener's cottage, followed by a hail of shot richocheting off the tiles. The terrified gardener bolted his door, believing he was under siege.

Under normal circumstances, the standard excuse Robin should employ when he is too slow to shoot a bird is '. . . too small'. In November, the first frost makes the birds fill their feathers and look bigger, and it carries the convincing ring of experience. Excuses such as, 'I trapped my finger in the Range Rover door', or 'How can anyone shoot properly with all that shouting going on?' should be strenuously avoided.

Bird lovers will be gratified to learn that there are enough poor shots around to ensure that their feathered friends have an enjoyable outing.

A pheasant disturbed in Wrabness Wood, Essex, made an

awayday of it by flying through a barrage of guns into the open window of a passing train. It travelled first class all the way to Harwich, where it was seen to alight and scuttle down the platform. Unfortunately it did not have a return ticket, and a porter cornered it and took it home for dinner.

For any reasonable gun, missing a bird gives rise to frustration rather than embarrassment. Whatever thoughts are steaming under your brown Derby, it is wise to say nothing. At a grouse shoot late in the season a guest loosed six barrels at a score of birds bearing down on him, without managing to ruffle a single feather. Rooted with rage he shook his fist furiously after the disappearing birds and screamed: 'Wait till my brother Tom comes next week. He'll tickle your tails for you!'

Grouse always have good reason to celebrate when foreigners are on the moor. Invest in a bullet-proof vest that does not ruin the cut of your tweeds if trigger-happy French, Italians or Belgians are about.

An understanding host, anxious to encourage a distinguished, but completely hopeless, French guest, escorted him to the remotest butt. After suggesting that he tried his hand at anything that came over, he returned at the end of the first drive and asked him how he had fared.

'The grouse, they fly too swift,' he shrugged. Then, brightening, he added: 'But of the *moutons sauvages* I have killed five . . .'

Nature's revenge on the grouse gun lies in the fact that the easiest bags have a habit of being the most unpalatable. Only the partially sighted could miss a big capercaillie as it crashes along, leaving a swathe of demolished fir trees. However, the gun's initial flush of pride rapidly turns puce at the dinner-table—grilled gumboots would be more digestible. A gamekeeper who was once asked by a guest how to tenderize an ancient cock capercaillie, advised him first to bury it in the ground for a month. 'Then,' he said to the chap listening avidly, 'the best thing you can do is forget where you buried him.'

This sporting strife

One of the drawbacks of country-house weekends is that people take games embarrassingly seriously. They play tennis in studied desperation, bridge with poker-faces – and at croquet they cheat.

Never give a dowager duchess an even break on the croquet-lawn – she will take you to the cleaners, feigning deafness when she bends the rules, and moving the ball the second you turn round to admire the topiary. Only a complete fool or a confirmed townie would believe that the old dear is happy to send her ball into the rhubarb, and retire for a cucumber sandwich, after ten minutes' play. Anyone over sixty-five who can whack a 1 lb ball the length of a lawn with a 3 lb mallet is not to be underestimated. And unless you are Hurlingham standard, decline any invitations to side-bets. All in all, croquet before Sunday lunch with frail, elderly ladies can only lead to chronic indigestion.

Unlike Californians, who sensibly use swimming-pools as an excuse for drinking and acquiring a tan, Green Wellies are dauntingly physical. They scream uproariously, sit on people's heads, swim very earnestly and remain underwater for alarmingly long periods (or not long enough, in some cases). And never ever believe anyone who tells you that the water temperature is 'gorgeous'. If the house is freezing you can imagine what the pool will be like.

The daily *après*-lunch invitation to take the dogs for a walk may seem appealing—if you enjoy a five-mile yomp. Of course, there is the compensation of the scenery, but with owners increasingly forced to sell great chunks of land, even that can have its disadvantages. Princess Margaret, visiting friends with shrinking acreage, has been seen clumping round a nearby housing-estate for her constitutional.

And if the outdoor games seem daunting, the indoor games are far more so. Almost without exception they depend for success upon a hapless victim, whose self-control and good nature can be stretched to breaking point if he is unfamiliar with Green Wellie horseplay. And first-time guests obviously provide excellent targets.

The oldest in the book is the Funnel Game. The perpetrator shows off his skill at dropping a 10p coin, balanced on his forehead, into a newspaper funnel sticking out from his waistband. When the victim volunteers to have a go, he tilts back his head to balance the coin, and a jug of water is poured down the funnel into his trousers. 'Tairbly funny—we absolutely *killed* ourselves.' But, of course, if he couldn't see *that* coming a mile away, then he deserved all he got.

The follow-up is to press a fiver into a grateful victim's palm and tell him he can keep it, if you can crack two eggs on his head. You crack one, take back the money and say you realize it can't be done. 'A hoot—rairly, rairly funny.'

Moriarty provides one of the few splendid opportunities for revenge. Players are blindfolded, and lie on the floor armed with rolled-up newspapers. The first asks: 'Are you there, Moriarty?' When his opponent replies, 'I am here', the questioner quickly computes the precise location of his head and scores by whacking it with the newspaper. A brass poker wrapped in a copy of *The Times* is a wonderful equalizer.

A fishy business

Hook, line and stinkers

One of life's most exhilarating vertical experiences is to fish for salmon on the tumbling, broad-bosomed rivers of Britain.

Each Spring—as the sap rises in the most perished Uniroyal waders—the migration of thousands of noble creatures is an awe-inspiring sight. Gleaming in the dawn light, they flash and weave on the epic journey north, up the M1 to Scotland. Unlike the majestic salmon, however, Robin and Nicky would never go through hell, high water and the risk of dramatic death just for sex.

Saab Turbos and BMWs bristling with Hardy's rod racks drift across the carriageways with driver fatigue. Dour traffic cops in chequered caps reel them in when the blood sugar level plummets after the final slice of quiche. Only seasoned salmon fishermen—with megaclamps holding twenty rods across the Range Rover roof—plough on like tank battalions across the border, courteously saluted by the local constabulary.

When you consider the number of people now discovering salmon fishing for the first time, it is surprising that there are still no lone green wellies to be found littering the roads north. Perhaps, terrified of losing their vital accessories, they carry them in welded trunks. Or even drive the 300 miles in their Hunters.

Most of them are drawn by the lure of those great rivers, the Tay and Spey. Hardier annuals push further north to Queen Mum country – the Dee, Helmsdale and Brora, and the distant hills of Achentoul.

Green wellies sprout like Astroturf along the Tay; a challenging river and – for the less intrepid – a haven where impressive catches can be obligingly arranged. In a good season the ghillies are as overworked as doormen at a Harrods sale. Arrivistes and geriatric generals adore it; once the tiresome problem of fishing is dispensed with, everyone can get down to the serious business of social drinking.

Over the years, with a river too wide to cover from the bank, Tay fishermen have evolved the art of boat fishing. Gone are the days of sweating ghillies struggling with oars to hold frail craft against a wilful current, while lantern-jawed John Buchan-types puff a pipe of Sobranie in the stern. The air is filled with the roar of expensive Evinrude eggbeaters powering boats that are dangerously over-loaded with monogrammed, Brady tackle-bags.

Salmon, to everyone's eternal gratitude, have a strong bent for self destruction. The king of the river will swallow just about anything, provided that it is presented in the right place at the right time, from Mother's Pride to a truffle tin. Although one and all will strenuously deny that they ever use anything other than a fly.

And they can be obliging in other ways as well. Lady Evelyn Cotterell recounts, in *Salmon Fishing on the Spey*, that her sister, Lady Percy, was being rowed across the river, when a 15-pounder cleared the water and crashed struggling into the lap of her skirt. Lady Percy, displaying admirable presence of mind, clasped it tightly to her heaving bosom, where it expired; presumably from shock.

First catch your ghillie

A ghillie is a man who will step on to the spot you have just vacated in disgust after a disastrous day, and land three obese salmon in ten minutes. To add insult to injury, he uses a line junked by some well-heeled visitor twenty years ago, and keeps his flies in a rusty Golden Virginia tin.

Ghillie-emulators try to position themselves downstream of a take, so the salmon has to pull against the current. An excited stockbroker once hooked a fish on the Dee and immediately splashed out of the water, heading hell for leather down the river bank, rod in hand.

'Where's he off to?' the bemused ghillie asked, leaning on his gaff.

'Getting below the salmon, of course,' the man's companion replied testily. They watched the flapping figure thunder into the distance, still trying to outpace the fish.

The ghillie shook his head in admiration at the olympian effort. 'If he can keep it up, he should be in Aberdeen for dinner,' he declared.

Some old ghillies are irrepressible ladies men, slipping hairy arms round slender waists to take the rod. 'Noo, ye should be holding it like this, madam'. Meanwhile male guests, struggling with a take, are dragged away downstream, cries for help ignored.

Willie the Ghillie–much loved by generations of Royals and still going strong–is a legend on the Brora. He has given years of helpful advice to lady anglers all at sea. Real Fishermen worship him.

Some ghillies overindulge the whisky in advanced years, but never lose a sharp eye for a tip, courteously removing an amateur's rod and getting him a take immediately. 'Your rod, sir,' they murmur, handing it back to the bungling fool, who proceeds to spend the next fifteen minutes doing his best to lose it. It is probably marginally more exciting than shopping at Fortnum's fish-counter, and leaves ample free time to invent tales of heroic tussles.

A ghillie can plant himself in a river as though his ancient waders were bolted to the gravel. Whereas many novices have difficulty mastering the knack of standing firm on slippery stones when waist-deep in a tumbling stream. As the water lifts them, they bob in a series of short pogo hops downstream, rolling the whites of their eyes. The good ghillie will grab a tuft of hair and bounce them back

Many novices have difficulty mastering the knack of standing firm on slippery stones when waist-deep in tumbling water.

again without a flicker. 'I think ye'd be better trying over here, sir.'

If a salmon takes the fly before the ghillie can intervene, the buoyant fisherman may take off like an olympic water skier. Ghillies have been known to cast after disappearing guests, and reel them in. Only iron self-control prevents the ultimate humiliation of throwing the gasping heap on to the scales and entering him in the house game-book.

I know of one retired military man who suffered the indignity of having to be gaffed by an Eskimo, not once, but twice as he floated down an Arctic river.

Nothing, however, beats a pair of chest-waders for assisting an undignified exit. A new type, fitted with an inflatable ring around the chest, is rapidly gaining popularity. The traditional version has a nasty habit, when a fisherman loses his footing, of flipping him upside down. The air in the loose chest and waist portion rushes to the feet, and it is not uncommon to see a pair of wildly-waving legs bob downstream.

I can recall only one occasion when the inscrutable mask of ghillie decorum has slipped. He was standing with his back to a cliff, fishing a loch from a narrow ledge. The local Presbyterian minister, a fanatical fly-fisherman, waited for an appropriate moment to apologetically squeeze past. As he edged across the ghillie's broad chest, he sensed a salmon below and, in a most unChristian gesture, cast his fly. Within seconds there was a swirl of water and a take. 'You bastard,' the ghillie wheezed in his ear. And the minister never spoke to him again for fifteen years.

Flies, and their undoing

Coarse fishermen—most aptly named—keep their maggots in Tupperware in the Frigidaire, and thaw them out on the riverbank by popping them into their mouths. This is a practice shunned by gentlemen, for obvious reasons—the lingering fumes of Highland Malt would render them senseless.

The Gentle Art demands a fly; not some mere pinch of navel fluff impaled on a hook, but a masterpiece of hair and steel. Retired army officers toil for hours in the glare of pre-war Anglepoise lamps, winding garish colour combinations that would give an interior decorator apoplexy. The fact that none even remotely resemble insects is a further indictment of the salmon's intelligence.

Real Fishermen dress their own flies, according to strict patterns named after pulp thrillers–Gold Murderer, Willie Gun, Thunder and Lightning–whereas townies buy them over the counter at Hardy's. A Stoat's Tail is a trusty favourite, made from dyed squirrel fur. Of course, Real Fishermen prefer to catch their own stoats, tracking them for three days across frozen tundra, and killing them with their bare hands, to snip off the vital tuft.

Some people make the mistake of parading about with Silver Doctors and Hairy Marys jabbed in the crowns of their fore and afts. They choose the biggest, gaudiest flies, but there must be a lot of explaining to do back at Moss Bros on Monday. Flies refuse to budge from tweed hats, leaving great holes torn in the tweed by panic-stricken wearers.

A fishing waistcoat, with a square of wool stitched to the breast, is the fashionable parking place for a discreet assortment of Dusty Millers and Jock Scotts. Hardy's catalogue is awash with them these days, but Real Fishermen always know an old lady in the village who runs them up for a fiver.

Top people make the pilgrimage to Brora to purchase flies from the diminutive Miss Megan Boyd, who ties for HRH and the Queen Mother. She is fond of tying a perfect fly at her cottage in the twinkling of an eye, and asking with a smile: 'Now, how much d'ye think?' Americans, horrified at the thought of getting them wet, take them home and mount them in blocks of perspex resin.

The only weapon worthy of priming with a Megan Boyd is a thirty-year-old Hardy split-cane rod. Real Fishermen swear that split-cane has a *feel* to it. The top section of a good split-cane rod is always supplied with a spare; fishing lore has it that the top cane, along with its owner, should be laid to rest after a hard day on the river. Lightweight carbon-fibre models are still regarded in some circles with suspicion, along with decimalization, electric blankets and socialism.

Real Fishermen dress their own flies.

But even the finest equipment can do little to remove the uncertainty of fishing. Half the joy of the Gentle Art lies in the unexpected. One fisherman, casting in the still air of twilight, had a take almost as soon as his fly touched the shining water. Amazed, he played it furiously, watching as the line sped to the opposite bank with a breathtaking turn of speed. Then it rocketed out of the water and into the undergrowth – attached to the backside of an equally surprised rat.

The novice always addresses the river with one of two techniques:

The *Indiana Jones,* in which the rod is twirled like a lariat weighted with two pounds of scrap iron. The fly crashes into the stream, adorned with freshly-plucked nettle clumps, assorted headgear and the sleeve of Pippa's Husky.

The other is the *Jimmy Chipperfield,* or ringmaster method, often posing greater threat to the caster himself than to his companions. The rod is cracked in a whiplash, sending the line hurtling first in the opposite direction to the river. Few return. It either catches a branch, dragging the amateur on to his back – or catapults forward snatching off his hairpiece on the way. 'Damned unusual fly you've got there, old man.'

The mortification can be even more excruciating. A few years ago a Northern businessman managed to impale a Cinnamon Turkey in the side of his head. He was carried to the corrugated-iron outpatients department of a Highland hospital and plonked in a chair to await the doctor. In the poorly-heated waiting-room his companions thoughtfully wrapped a tartan travelling rug around his shoulders. As he sat there moaning, with a variety of beads and feathers jutting out from his head, two elderly ladies were heard earnestly debating which clan he might be chief of.

In the heat of the night

The ultimate in fishing one-upmanship is sea-trouting, a pastime totally baffling to outsiders. Its followers fish forceful trout streams at night, in pitch darkness, without the hint of a light; an occupation best suited to members of the SAS, or the excessively shy.

Old hands can 'feel' the fly, play a trout and land it, without seeing a thing. It has its advantages. Dress is entirely optional, and anyone lacking the right kit for conventional fly fishing, but with a good line in conversation, might find it attractive. Mind you, the social side is hardly frenzied. A friend of mine once recognized the voice of a fellow dinner-party guest as a man he had fished with regularly for four years.

Novices thankfully overlook such esoteric pleasures, which is surprising, as tales of The One That Got Away can be embroidered without fear of contradiction.

The problem with sea trouting is the ones that don't. One dark night on the Lune, beneath a bomber's moon, an excited voice suddenly cried: 'God, it's enormous! Look out—I'm coming through.' A shadowy figure was seen splashing heavily downstream, his reel zipping and whining furiously. 'He's a big beggar,' the voice gasped to each solitary fisherman as he passed. Until one, blessed with better eyesight than the rest, snorted: 'You've hooked a tree trunk, you bloody fool . . .'

It is doubtful whether the motley, eccentric brotherhood of sea-trouters would stand scrutiny in the cold light of day. Midnight fishing lends itself to bizarre dress habits, which have, on rare occasions, been exposed.

One coal-black night on the river, a veteran sea-trouter was heard to whisper desperately for assistance. Intrigued, a nearby fisherman waded over to find that his neighbour had cast a fly through the lobe of his own ear. At 2 am they presented themselves under the fluorescent lights of the local infirmary, looking like tramps on a spree in an Oxfam shop. The victim, a distinguished Peer of the Realm, was staggering, one arm flung round his companion's shoulder, with a scarlet Cardinal dangling from his ear in all its feathered glory.

The ultimate in one-upmanship is sea-trouting. Its followers fish forceful troutstreams at night, in pitch darkness, without the hint of a light.

Super japes and wizard wheezes

There are two types of people in this life: those who fall about helplessly when they recall practical jokes, and those who regard them as about as funny as having a boil lanced.

The best pranks are those quietly undone by a third party, which lead to great confusion at breakfast. The apple-pie bed, wickedly put right by the host and hostess, is a nice touch. 'Sleep alright, then?' asks the perpetrator innocently. 'Perfectly, thank you,' the victim replies, faintly puzzled. A sheep in the bed is a house-party favourite, along with lobsters, or anything which slithers or wriggles. The game is often given away by a pyramid of sniggers outside the bedroom door.

A well-planned jape is almost an art-form in itself. Some guests take studious delight in preparing the most complex scenarios to produce maximum discomfort and embarrassment.

A classic of its type concerned a grumpy old deer stalker in Sutherland who was well-known for his obsessive hatred of Germans. A mischievous party, noting the arrival of ten Bavarian businessmen on the hill, decided to rev him up. They informed the Germans, kitted in feathered Tyrolean trilbies, that they had been assigned the best stalker on the estate, and would do well to implicitly obey his every command.

The stalker, to his deep disgust, was told that he had been assigned not the usual one or two guests, but a squad of former Wehrmacht officers. He ranted, raved and at one stage refused point blank. The party sympathized, but insisted that it was the laird's orders. They sat on a wall in great glee watching the stalker—face set like an approaching thunderstorm—march off, with the Bavarians humming in Indian file behind.

At dusk the new arrivals staggered back exhausted and be-draggled. They had been taken on a twenty-six mile route march, carefully planned to ensure that the most they saw of a red deer was from a distance of two miles through powerful binoculars. As the ghillie stomped off to his croft to erase the experience with a bottle of whisky, the leader of the party called: 'That was wonderful. We will go again tomorrow, ja?'

Some wizard wheezes are considered hilarious on a sliding scale of distaste. The more revolting the result, the greater the mirth.

Typical of this was a group of guests week-ending in a fine old country house by the sea. They decided to take a boat out to do some fishing, using conger eel as bait. After several hours they returned empty-handed, but felt obliged to take something back to the house for their efforts. The very ugly, yard-long conger, with a few inches of its tail missing, was tipped into a large plastic bag. It was not only bloody and slimy but, having probably been caught the previous day, it smelled like a dozen tomcats in a wrestler's laundry-bag. Back at the house, everyone who peeped into the bag was utterly revolted. When the fun wore off, the question was what on earth to do with it—at the same time providing maximum discomfort to a member of the house party.

The conger was hauled to the room of a Harley Street doctor, who was lying on his bed enjoying an afternoon nap. The fishing party tiptoed in, and were debating in whispers where to place it for optimum effect, when he began to wake. Hurriedly they drag-ged it through to the Victorian bathroom, and dumped it into the ornate lavatory pan. The matelots made their escape, leaving the doctor deep in sleep again.

Five minutes later, his wife briskly entered from an invigorating constitutional and headed straight for the bathroom. For about thirty seconds there was an uncanny silence, followed by hysterical screaming. The poor woman had to be tranquillized for the rest of the day with an injection from her husband's medical bag.

She caught an early plane home, convinced that the monster had been living in the garden cesspit, and had slithered through the labyrinth of antique plumbing to attack her. She is understood never to have ventured out of Belgravia since.

Infinitely more entertaining, perhaps, was the barrister who spent two weeks at a fishing lodge, with a recipe for the perfect holiday. At the end of the first week his attractive girlfriend would leave for home–to be replaced by girlfriend number two. Timing was essential, but the train tickets were booked, and timetables memorized to cover every mishap British Rail could engineer.

His host, unfortunately, had a devilish sense of humour, and at the appropriate time announced that the train had been derailed. The girl was naturally disappointed–but all was not lost. The host had telephoned the local airport and would be delighted to pay her air fare back to London . . . if she would care to stay another night.

The barrister spluttered and protested, but his girlfriend insisted that it was most generous and kind, and delightedly accepted. The unfortunate brief had neither the means of escape nor mitigating circumstances. He spent breakfast like a condemned man and, to the delight of his friends, grew visibly pale as a taxi swept into the drive to disgorge a girl even more stunning than the first.

His original plan was finally effected, but not without a degree of violence. Walking was painful for a few days, but his injuries were happily not permanent.

One jape, brilliantly planned and executed by friends, has now passed into the slim volume of Green Wellie humour. The main instigators were David Hampson-Smith, a deer-stalking man of uncanny skill, and the sprightly figure of Lt.-Col. Gilbert Chaldecott, who once managed to take four salmon in the middle of a NATO exercise. They were spurred on by Alister Reid, veteran host of splendid house parties.

They were staying at Uppart House, owned by the Countess of

Sutherland, when news filtered through of another house party on the estate some miles away. Beaulieu Castle had been taken by the international rich– English, American and French–whose Lear jets littered the grounds as they prepared to embark on a week's wining, dining, salmon fishing and stag shooting.

With the colonel acting as a dour Scots telephone operator, Hampson-Smith rang the host at the castle and announced, in a broad Lancashire accent, that he was Tommy Arkwright, chairman of Accrington Working Men's Club Coarse Fishing Section. His lads–seventeen of them–had booked the castle for the week, and were on their way by minibus. There was a moment's silence, and before the distinguished host could reply, operator Chaldecott cut him off.

The Beaulieu party, who were planning to fly to the Bahamas after an idyllic week, regarded the prospect of a double booking as a minor irritation. But when Hampson-Smith rang again the following day, niggling doubts began to set in.

'Sorry we'll be late, owd lad,' he chattered breezily. 'Minibus had a blow-out, but we're on our way again. See you tomorrow, chook.' Click.

The worried host was by this time stiffening with apprehension, wondering how to extricate himself from an appalling situation.

The third call came the next evening, timed for the middle of dinner. Accrington Workingmen's Club announced that they were half an hour's drive away. The only answer was the local constabulary.

'Where are you now, my dear fellow,' Beaulieu Castle asked cautiously.

'In the station car park having our butties.'

'Good. Now you just wait there, and we'll get someone out to talk to you ...'

'No time for that, owd lad,' breezed Hampson-Smith, wary of the ploy. 'We're all off for a pint. The pubs have just opened. See you later, chook.' Click.

The hoaxers, unable to resist consolidating the victory, motored to the floodlit castle, a little unsure of what to expect. Two Scottish housekeepers ushered them through numerous ballrooms and corridors to the doors of an immense dining-room and announced them. Thirty English and Americans pushed back their chairs from a table laden with silver and crystal. The French looked totally baffled.

Hampson-Smith waded into a long monologue about maggots and blow-outs to stunned silence. Then the colonel rose to his feet and, unable to sustain a suitable accent, announced that he was proud to be president of the club. These working class chaps were the salt of the earth and had his full support in what was clearly their rightful booking.

Uppart House, unable to keep a straight face, finally confessed. There was shouting, cheering and table-thumping—as much from relief as appreciation. The French stood in unison and politely applauded.

Lying low – the art of deer stalking

The only time you are ever likely to see a member of the aristocracy on his hands and knees is when the Chateau Lafite has been an exceptionally good year – or when he is following his stalker. A laird may disappear for a day's sport without his ghillie but, in the stag season, he is rarely seen without his nose a few inches from his head stalker's backside.

After a lifetime out in the wilds managing deer, stalkers are a law unto themselves. Ferocious, granite-hard ex-Lovat Scouts who have killed men with their bare hands – and may again if you ignore their advice.

The great appeal of deer stalking is that, having crawled upwind, soaking wet and covered in midge-bites, there is only you and the stalker alone on the hill. And no-one will ever know what a cock-up you made of it – provided, of course, that the tip is big enough.

Stealth is essential. Even if you disturb a sheep or grouse, this can alert a stag a mile away. And when you have inched yourself on your belly for two miles through a peat bog, and the alarm on your digital watch goes off, only hard cash can save you from an unthinkable end. Deer have a highly-tuned sense of hearing. If your nose is dripping like a tap down your new sweater from Gurnseys Galore – don't even sniff.

All need not be lost, though. Exasperated stalkers have been known to wrench a .303 from the hands of a snivelling rifle and dispatch the beast themselves. And, with a rustle of grateful fivers, nothing more will be said. An extra pound or two is necessary to buy the pony boy a pint but, thankfully for the rotten shot, fewer estates employ them nowadays. Under EEC kill-and-chill regulations all venison destined for the market has to be inspected and frozen within twenty-four hours. As the embarrassed Robin lies in the heather, concocting a suitable after-dinner story, the stalker whips a walkie-talkie from his tweeds. 'Come in, Angus. Are ye receiving, Angus? Wake up, damn ye . . .' And with a mighty roar the Argocat lunges over the hill and drags away the evidence.

Deer stalking is physically very demanding. Probably the first thing to strike the novice on arriving in a deer forest is that there isn't a tree in sight; just miles of bare, gale-lashed moor where commandoes go to pass out—from exposure. The prospect of being dragged twenty miles to the nearest infirmary behind a Snocat is a daunting thought. It is, however, traditional for the stalker to carry your rifle—in case you die from exhaustion, thereby denying him his tip.

When the late Lord Strathnairn was in advanced years, he once became so tired after the first few miles that he waved his stalkers ahead to spy for deer. They returned to find the old chap sleeping blissfully beneath a boulder. The head stalker slung him over his shoulder, still snoring, and carried him up the hill to the firing position.

Before leaving the house, around 9 am, you will have an opportunity to target-test your rifle in the grounds. Put in months of practice in the office bagging flies with elastic bands, because the real purpose is to test you.

The ability to hit something is quite an advantage as most highland landowners suffer from acute insecurity of tenure, and deer are one of their few hopes of remaining solvent. If you knock the weather-vane off the stable roof, it can be a long walk back to the station.

Free stalking is enjoyed by only a privileged handful with the

No-one will ever know what a cock-up you made of it —providing, of course, that the tip is big enough.

means to reciprocate. A single squeeze of the trigger can set anyone else back about £100 + VAT. A royal or imperial, heavily sought after for the trophy rooms of German and Italian industrialists, costs around £2000. So mere mortgaged mortals must ensure they are reasonable shots. There is a statutory forfeit of £15 for wounding a stag—or the whole cost of the venison if it limps away uncaught—which is enough to give any townie a nasty case of trigger tremble.

Even old hands can make a hash of it. One experienced lady rifle of my acquaintance, who shall remain nameless, fumbled desperately with the bolt in an attack of stag fever. 'Oh, fuck me!' she exploded.

'Madam,' breathed the stalker furiously. 'Make up your bloody mind—d'ye want to make love, or shoot the beast . . .'

As for dress, the wise wear tweed plus-twos with thermal underwear to repel the moisture. Scotland, for the uninitiated, can be as damp as the Atlantic. Novices go for Barbour Solways, which rustle less, and tout Gray telescopes made from Japanese aluminium. Take an old brass Ross or Hilary-Everest scope with you if you can find one; it may drag your shoulder off after ten miles, but at least it looks as though you've done it before. For more impressive results, remove the lens cap before scanning for deer. A well-worn thumbstick is handy for steadying the rifle in woodland stalking. But no matter how carefully-distressed the accessories, only a keen eye and a sure hand can win a stalker's grudging esteem.

The unwitting first-timer provides a grizzled stalker with his best sport of the day. The wind-up seldom varies. After an intimidating do-as-I-do lecture, he strikes off for the position on his hands and knees, up the middle of a raging burn. The hapless novice, teeth chattering, obediently follows, frantically trying to recall if his BUPA instalments are paid up. Strict rules of silence forbid complaining. If he as much as emits a stifled whimper, the stalker will spread his arms, building a wall of water, which he releases to sweep the screaming guest downstream.

Germans refuse point-black even to kneel in the heather for fear

Germans are smooth bores of the highest calibre, but irritatingly good shots.

of ruining their tweeds. They are smooth bores of the highest calibre, but irritatingly good shots. Former Wehrmacht officers, in particular, have a habit of enthusiastically producing motor-drive Leicas to take colour pictures as the stag is gralloched.

Such is the unpredictable nature of deer stalking, that even the best shots can have their guns spiked. Nicholas Courtney tells, in *Sporting Royals*, of the long hard day Prince Philip spent crawling after a stag at Balmoral. At nightfall, soaking wet and exhausted, he finally managed to get it in his sights. Just as the beast was rising, two teenagers in orange anoraks sauntered into view. When Prince Philip enquired their business, they replied: 'Sorry Sir—we're on the Duke of Edinburgh's Award Scheme.'

Marching orders

However delightful the company, there comes a time when even the most immovable guest has to leave. When polite hints fail, drastic measures may be resorted to. One crusty host would simply throw the mains switch, plunging the entire house into darkness, and retire to bed.

This is one of the very few occasions when living on an island can have its advantages. Lord St Leven, at St Michael's Mount, has the trump card of high tides, which swamp the causeway, cutting off his home each evening. The owner of an island castle on the west coast of Scotland confided that he arranges a fake telephone call, warning of approaching squalls, an hour before the last ferry is due to leave.

But the threat of being cut off from the known world can seriously backfire. The 10th Duke of Arran, a warmly generous man, would give his guests a docket, enabling them to explore the island, staying and eating wherever they chose at his expense. Several, enchanted by the splendid isolation and bracing air, put down roots and stayed for the rest of their lives.

A favourite ploy elsewhere in Scotland is to station a piper on the parapets at dawn on the morning of departure. Guests loathe it, but it works.

From time to time there are those whose OTT behaviour necessitates them being asked to leave—hopefully, never to return.

Circumstances range from being caught inflagrante with the hostess's daughter (score 10), chopping up a Chippendale bedroom chair for firewood (8½), or urinating in a Shibayama vase when losing your bearings (5).

The most frequently-told story, now firmly part of Green Wellie lore, concerns the guest whose arm flopped out of bed in his sleep and sent a glass of water flying from the bedside table. He threw back the soaking bed linen, and stumbled across the room, feet squelching on the carpet, to grope along the wall for the light switch. It clicked on to illuminate a scene of utter devastation. What he had imagined to be a tumbler was, in fact, a very full inkstand.

The host of a fly-fishing party recalled an occasion when two ladies had to be ordered home for excessive drunkeness. Despite a marginal interest in field sports, they had insisted on accompanying their husband and boyfriend on the trip. Quickly finding that the north of Scotland has little to offer in the way of social life, they turned to vodka.

Each morning, in the early hours, they rolled back to the lodge from the nearest hotel, fifteen miles away, singing loudly and waking up the household. On the fourth day they wrote off their Alfa, blocking a single track road across the moor, and completely cutting off a nearby village. After knocking on the door of every Presbyterian croft for assistance, they arrived with their Xavier Danaud shoes falling off, singing a medley of the Rolling Stones greatest hits.

It was time to go. Their mild-mannered host, goaded beyond endurance, and facing the wrath of the local population, told them they would have to leave the next morning. They plunged into another hog-whimperer, giggling in delight—there was no way they *could* go, the road was jammed and the car was a write-off.

Next day their determined host bundled them into a Land-Rover, drove across soberingly rough country, and slithered to a halt at a remote stretch of railway track. As he glanced at his pocket watch, a rumbling of heather indicated the arrival of the early passenger train to Inverness. Boldly he stepped on to the line and, raising his arm, commanded it to stop. When the train screeched and clanked to a standstill in a shower of sparks, he threw them aboard, tipped the driver and waved him on . . .

The Green Wellie year

A table of movable feasts

January: Put the garden on a critical path analysis. End-of-season cock shoots.

February: Hang 'em high—pheasant, woodcock and partridge shooting ends. Mudlarks—point-to-pointing starts.

March: First ripples on the salmon rivers. Brush down the Derby—flat racing opens. Cheltenham National Hunt Festival.

April: Hunting season ends—hang up the pink. Cricket, polo gets underway. Grand National. Veg. in for the self-sufficient. Badminton (the Anne and Mark show). Debs. Stag shooting ends in England on the 30th.

May: First onset of tennis fever. Cast off—river trout fishing begins.

June: Royal Ascot. Epsom. The Derby. Hunters on for soggy agricultural shows.

July: 1st: stag hunting crawls to life in Scotland. Croquet Open, Hurlingham. The Game Fare—mass parade of Green Wellies. Glorious Goodwood.

August: 1st: English stag season begins. Have bird, will travel—the Glorious Twelfth. Ptarmigan and snipe shooting also gets underway.

September: Cock left—partridge shooting starts. Cricket bats and croquet mallets away for the winter. Burghley Horse Trials. St Leger. Newmarket.

October: 1st: blast off for pheasant and woodcock. Salmon fishing ends. Trout fishing ends. Beagling begins. Horse of the Year Show. 20th: Scottish stag shooting ends. Last of the orchard apples.

November: Autumn mist and aerosols—hunting starts.

December   10th: Grouse season ends. Useful Christmas presents. Boxing Day meets.

County counselling

Gun lore, horsey drop-ins and useful addresses in the shires

AVON

Shooting
1. The Spa Shooting Grounds, I. M. Crudgington Ltd, Gun-makers, Green Street, Bath.
2. Lady's Wood Shooting School, Maple Ridge Lane, Horton, Chipping Sodbury, Bristol.

BEDFORDSHIRE

The Royal Society For The Protection of Birds: The Lodge, Sandy, where small Green Wellies enjoy a gander.
Shooting
Duglan and Cooper Ltd, Church Street, Dunstable.

BERKSHIRE

Point-to-point
The Old Berks Hunt at Lockinge, Nr Wantage. Old Berks on sticks watch young berks sail over them.

Shooting
Pennsport Ltd, Thames Valley Shooting Ground, Tomb Farm, Upper Basildon, Nr Pangbourne, Berks.
Show Jumping
Winkfield.

BORDERS

Point-to-points
1. Friars Haugh, Kelso.
2. Mosshouses, Galashiels. Watch out for the weather.

BUCKINGHAMSHIRE

Point-to-points
1. Kimble, Aylesbury.
2. Little Horwood, Nr Bletchley. High point of the stockbroker-belt season.

CAMBRIDGESHIRE

Point-to-points
1. Cottenham, Nr Cambridge. A five-wellie rating. People sacrifice a tenner to get their name on the Cambridgeshire Harriers Saddling Box Fund donations list.
2. Horseheath, Linton.

CHESHIRE

The Wildfowlers' Association of Great Britain and Ireland: 104 Watergate Street, Chester. Range Rovers bristle with their stickers.
Point-to-points
1. Alpraham, Tarporley.
2. Eaton Hall. Nr Chester. Equestrian lift-off at the Duke of Westminster's private airfield.

3. Tatton Park, Knutsford. Horsey Manchester industrialists.
Shooting
North Wales Shooting School, Sealand Manor, Chester.

CORNWALL

Point-to-points
1. Crimp, Nr Bude.
2. Lemalla, Nr Launceston.
3. Tehidy, Camborne.
4. Wadebridge, Trewornan Farm.
Cornish peter-pees are hearty affairs; robust eccentrics abound.
Shooting
1. Lower Lake Shooting Ground, Upton Cross, Liskeard, Cornwall.
2. Southern Gun Company, Market Street, Bodmin, Cornwall.

CUMBRIA

Point-to-point
Dalston, Nr Carlisle. Flocks of Green Wellies drive down from the hills.

DERBYSHIRE

Point-to-point
Flagg Moor, Nr Buxton.

DEVONSHIRE

Point-to-points
More cream than Cornwall, but slightly clotted.
1. Bishopsleigh, Nr Crediton.
2. Bratton Down, Nr Barnstaple.
3. Flete Park, Ermington, Nr Plymouth.
4. Galmpton, Brisham.

5. Kilworthy, Tavistock.
6. Ottery St Mary, Bishopscourt.
7. Stafford Cross, Seaton.
8. Thorverton, Nr Exeter.
9. Totnes.
10. Umberleigh, Nr Barnstaple.

Shooting
1. North Devon Shooting School, East Street, South Molton, North Devon.
2. Drum Sports, Courtney Street, Newton Abbot, Devon.

DORSET

Point-to-points
1. Badbury Rings, Nr Blandford.
2. Toller Down Gate, Beaminster.

DUMFRIES AND GALLOWAY

Point-to-point
Lockerbie, Roberthill.

DURHAM

Point-to-point
Witton Castle, Bishop Auckland.

DYFED

Point-to-points
1. Erw Lon, Nr Carmarthen.
2. Lydstep, Tenby.
3. Scoveston Fort, Milford Haven.

ESSEX

Point-to-point
Marks Tey, Nr Colchester. One of Cortinaland's few Green Wellie occasions.

FIFE

Point-to-point
Balcormo Mains, Leven. Clan gathering of Scottish Green Wellies.

MID GLAMORGAN

Point-to-point
Nelson, Pontypridd.

SOUTH GLAMORGAN

Point-to-points
1. St Hilary, Cowbridge.
2. St Mary Hill, Bridgend.

GLOUCESTERSHIRE

The Greenest Wellies in England.
Point-to-points
1. The Beaufort, Didmarton. *Very* Green Wellie. Patronized by Royals and the very rich.
2. Young farmers abandon end-of-year accounts for the Ledbury Hunt, Maisemore Park.
3. Siddington, Cirencester.
4. Springhill, Broadway.
5. Woodford, Dursley.
Then wing over to:
 The Hawk Trust, The Falconry Centre, Nr Newent.
(Ask why most falconers are vegetarians?)

and:
Wildfowl Trust, The New Grounds, Slimbridge—
to collect posters for young Green Wellie bedroom walls.

GWENT

Point-to-points
1. Bassaleg, Newport.
2. Howick, Chepstow.
3. Llanvapley, Abergavenny, where Green Wellies sprout like leeks.

Shooting
D. J. Litt (Firearms) Ltd, Unit 3, Maesglas Industrial Estate, Newport, Gwent.

HAMPSHIRE

Point-to-points
1. Aldershot; brings out the army.
2. Hackwood Park, Basingstoke.
3. Tweseldown–RMA Sandhurst's Draghunt.

Shooting
1. Game Conservancy, Burgate Manor, Fordingbridge, Hants.
2. Game Farmers' Association, Micheldever, Winchester, Hants.
3. Herriard Sporting Guns, Alton Road, Herriard.

HEREFORDSHIRE

Point-to-points
1. Brampton Bryan, Nr Ludlow.
2. Bredwardine, Nr Hay-on-Wye.
3. Cursneh Hill, Leominster.
4. Garnons, Nr Hereford.
5. Upper Sapey, Nr Bromyard.
6. Whitwick, Newtown, Nr Hereford.

Herefordshire point-to-points have a reputation for being friendly, sociable and great fun.

HERTFORDSHIRE

Polo
Woolmers Park.
Shooting
Regent Shooting Ground, Rowley Green, Herts.

HUMBERSIDE

Shooting
Bygot Wood Shooting Ground, J. Wheater (Gunmakers) Ltd, Anlaby Road, Hull.
Point-to-point
Dalton Park, Nr Beverley.

KENT

Old Green Wellies make the pilgrimage to the Buffs Museum. The old Third of Foot is fondly remembered by the not-so-fleet of foot.
Point-to-points
1. Aldington, Nr Ashford.
2. Charing, Nr Ashford.
3. Detling, Maidstone.
4. Penshurst, Tonbridge.
Shooting
1. Greenfield's Shooting School, Upper Bridge Street, Canterbury, Kent.
2. Saddlery and Gun Room, Main Road, Biggin Hill, Kent.

LANCASHIRE

The British Deer Society, The Deer Museum, Low Hay Bridge, Bouth by Ulveston, Lancs.

Point-to-points
1. Gisburn.
2. Whittington, Kirby Lonsdale.
Shooting
1. Kelbrook Shooting School, The Shooting Lodge, Kelbrook Moor.
2. Ray Fox Guns, Bolton Street, Chorley.

LEICESTERSHIRE

Point-to-point
Garthorpe, Nr Melton Mowbray. Tairbly Green Wellie. The Quorn, the Cottesmore and the Belvoir—if you can't afford to hunt with them, see them take a tumble.

LINCOLNSHIRE

Point-to-points
1. Brocklesby Park, Nr Grimsby.
2. Carholme, Lincoln.
Shooting
1. Elderkins Gunmakers, Spalding.
2. Peter Coppin, Gun Dealer, Willoughby, Alford.

GREEN WELLIE LONDON

Arms and Armour Society, Great James Street, Holborn, WC1.
British Field Sports Society, Caxton Street, SW1.
Clay Pigeon Shooting Association, Eley Estate, Angel Road, N18.
Country Landowners' Association, Swallow Street, W1.
Country Life, Tavistock Street, Coventry Garden, WC2.
The Field, Stratton Street, W1.
Forestry Commission, Saville Row, W1X 2AY.
Guns Review, Ravenhill Publishing Co., City Road, EC1.
Kennel Club, Clarges Street, Piccadilly, W1.

Nature Conservancy, Belgrave Square, SW1.
Pax Guns Ltd, Archway Road, Highgate.
Royal Society for the Prevention of Cruelty to Animals, Jermyn Street, SW1.
Sporting Services International, Dover Street, W1.
St Hubert's Club, Hamilton Gardens, St John's Wood, NW1.

LOTHIAN

British Field Sports Society (Scotland), Haig House, Drumsheugh Garden, Edinburgh EH3 7RN.
Royal Society for the Protection of Birds (Scotland), Regent Terrace, Edinburgh.
Point-to-point
Oatridge, Uphall.

MERSEYSIDE

The Grand National, Aintree. Last bastion of beleaguered Scouse Green Wellies.
Shooting
Sporting Life, Church Road, Rainford, St Helens.

MIDDLESEX

Shooting
1. Guns&Tackle(Gunsmiths),HighStreet,Whitton,Twickenham.
2. Holland and Holland's Shooting School, Duckshill Road, Northwood, Mddx.
3. Muzzle Loaders' Association, Thames Street, Sunbury-on-Thames, Middx.
4. West London Shooting Grounds, Northolt, Mddx.

NORFOLK

Pheasant Trust, Hawks Hill, Great Witchingham, Norfolk.
Point-to-points
1. Costessey, Royal Norfolk Showground, Norwich.
2. Fakenham, N.H. course.

NORTHAMPTONSHIRE

Point-to-points
1. Dingley, Market Harborough.
2. Guilsborough, Nr Northampton.
3. Newton Bromswold, Rushden.

NORTHUMBERLAND

Point-to-points
1. Alnwick, Ratcheugh Farm.
2. Corbridge.
3. Tranwell, Morpeth.

NOTTINGHAMSHIRE

Point-to-point
Thorpe, Newark.

OXFORDSHIRE

Point-to-points
1. Heythrop, Chipping Norton. Smoothest of the Green Wellie gatherings. Good course. Natwest sponsored.
2. Kingston Blount, Watlington.
3. Mollington, Nr Banbury.

POWYS

Point-to-points
1. Llanfrynach, Brecon.
2. Talybont-on-Usk, Nr Brecon.

RENFREWSHIRE

Shooting
County Sports, Neilston Road, Paisley.

SHROPSHIRE

The Shrewsbury Show.
Point-to-points
1. Bitterley, Ludlow.
2. Eyton-on-Severn, Nr Shrewsbury.
3. Weston Park, Nr Telford.
Shooting
1. G. E. Turner (Gunsmith) Market Street, Wellington, Shropshire.
2. The West Midlands Shooting Grounds, Hodnet, Shropshire.
3. The Wrekin Shooting Ground, Wellington, Shropshire.

SOMERSET

Point-to-points
1. Cotley Farm, Chard.
2. Holnicote, Minehead.
3. Jordans, Ilminster.
4. Kingweston, Somerton.
5. Mounsey Hill Gate, Dulverton.
6. Nedge, Wells.
7. Williton, Watchet.

STRATHCLYDE

Point-to-point
Bogside, Irvine. Appropriately named on a bad day.

SUFFOLK

Point-to-points
1. Ampton, Nr Bury St Edmunds.
2. Higham, Nr Colchester.

SURREY

Point-to-point
Peper Harow, Godalming.
Shooting
1. Egham Gun Centre, High Street, Egham.
2. S. R. Jeffery and Son, High Street, Guildford.
3. Mitchell and Sons, Brighton Road, Coulston.

SUSSEX

Point-to-point
East Sussex and Romney Marsh, Broad Oak, Heathfield.
Polo
Cowdray Park. Low on Argie-bargy, high on Royals.
Shooting
1. The Chichester Armoury, Westgate, Chichester.
2. Diamond Guns, High Street, Heathfield.
3. The Sussex Gun Room, The Covert, East Street, Petworth.

STAFFORDSHIRE

Point-to-points
1. Hilton Park Arena, Essington.
2. The Meynell and S. Staffs Hunt, Sandon, Nr Stone, Staffs.

1. Garland Shooting Grounds, Raddle Farm, Edingale, Tamworth, Staffs.
2. M.B. Guns, Waterloo Street, Burton on Trent.

WARWICKSHIRE

Green Wellie sanctified ground:
The British Horse Society, Stoneleigh, Kenilworth, Warwicks.
Point-to-points
1. Lowsonford, Henley-in-Arden.
2. Clifton-on-Dunsmore, Midhurst.
Shooting
1. The Birmingham Gun Barrel Proof House, Banbury Street, Bmn 5.
2. The Gun Shop, Lawford Road, Rugby.
3. Sidelock Guns, Coleshill Road, Atherstone.

WEST MIDLANDS

Shooting
1. The Gun Trade Association, Chamber of Commerce House, Harborne Road, Edgbaston.
2. William Powell and Sons (Gunmakers) Ltd, Carrs Lane, Bmn 4.
3. Trapshot Ltd, High Street, Lye, Nr Stourbridge.
4. W & C Scott (Gunmakers) Ltd, Premier Works, Tame Rd, Witton, Bmn.

WILTSHIRE

Longleat, Warminster. Wiltshire's answer to the Waltons.
Point-to-point
Larkhill, Amesbury. Bleak in February. Fairly Army.
Shooting
1. Gamekeepers' Association (otherwise known as the sealed-lips club), Pentridge, Dorset, via Salisbury, Wilts.

2. Roses Wood Shooting Ground, Butter Cottage, Haugh, Winsley, Bradford on Avon, Wilts.

WORCESTERSHIRE

Point-to-points
1. North Ledbury Hunt, Ryall's Court, Upton-on-Severn.
2. The Worcestershire, Chaddesley Corbett. Superb point-to-pointing. Five wellie rating.

Shooting
Trapshot Ltd, Marina Arms, East Waterside, Upton-on-Severn, Worcs.

NORTH YORKSHIRE

Point-to-points
1. Charm Park, Wykenham, Scarborough.
2. Duncombe Park, Helmsley.
3. Easingwold, Nr York.
4. Hornby Castle, Catterick.
5. Hutton Rudby, Stokesley.
6. Little Ayton, Stokesley.
7. Wetherby, N.H. course, Nr Harrogate.
8. Whitewell-on-the-Hill, Nr Malton. Green Wellies rub shoulders with racing buffs for Lord Grimthorpe's Gold Cup. Underline heavily in diary.

Shooting
The Granery, North Rigton, Nr Harrogate.

WEST YORKSHIRE

Shooting
1. Holmfirth Shooting School, Edge End Farm, Nr Ford Inn, Holmfirth, Huddersfield.
2. J.P.S. Guns, Lower Warren Gate, Wakefield.